Easy Crafts for Children

by

Marcia Wolfe

illustrated by

Richard Briggs

STANDARD PUBLISHING

Cincinnati, Ohio

2154

ISBN 0-87239-844-7
Copyright © 1985. The STANDARD PUBLISHING Company,
Cincinnati, Ohio. A division of STANDEX INTERNATIONAL
Corporation.
Printed in U.S.A.

CONTENTS

To my sons Chad and Ryan and to all children

May they through these experiences be more sensitive
to the beauty of God's creation and better understand
their own uniqueness as children of God.

Spring Birds

Ages: 4-7
Materials:
Construction paper
Glue

Directions:
Cut two circles with 4″ diameters and one circle with a 2″ diameter. Use yellow paper for ducks and chicks. Brown or gray can be used for a robin. Fold both larger circles in half. Glue bottom halves (the body) of these two circles together. Slide the smaller circle (head) in between the two larger circles centering where the larger circles are folded. Fold top halves (the wings) away from each other. For ducks and chicks, cut legs and beak from orange paper and eyes from black paper. For the robin, cut a beak from yellow paper, eyes from black paper, and a breast from red paper.
Variation:
Make a raven from black paper; a dove from white paper; a quail from brown paper.

Daffodil

Ages: 5-8
Materials:
Construction paper: green, yellow, pastel shades
Glue

Directions:
Trace a pattern similar to the illustration onto yellow paper. Cut out daffodil shape. Fold up every other section to form the trumpet of the daffodil. Cut the stem and leaves from green paper. If desired, the flower can be mounted on an egg shape cut from pastel construction paper.

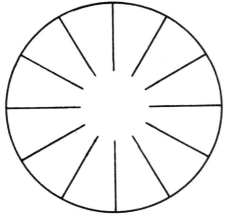

Robin

Ages: 5-10
Materials:
Construction paper: light blue, black, and yellow
Crayons
Milkweed pod with half of seeds removed
Cotton ball
Glue
Red tempera
Paper punch

Directions:
Paint the bottom fourth of a milkweed pod with red tempera. While the paint dries, draw a background for the bird on a piece of light blue paper. Cut a beak from yellow paper. Use a paper punch to cut a black eye. Glue eye and beak onto bird. Also, glue a cotton ball inside the pod. Glue the bird to the paper by gluing the cotton ball—not the pod—to the paper.
Variation:
For winter birds, follow above directions omitting the red tempera.

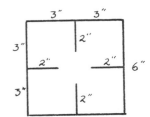

Tulip

Ages: 7-9
Materials:
Construction paper: green, red, yellow
Glue

Directions:
Cut the yellow or red paper into 6″ squares. Cut 2″ slits in the middle of each side. Form the paper into a cup shape by overlapping and gluing adjoining sections. Glue on a ¾″ strip of green paper for stem. Cut leaves from green paper, and glue to stem.

Pussy Willow

Ages: 4-7
Materials:
    Light blue construction paper
    Crayons: brown and green
    Yarn or ribbon
    Tempera
    Powdered laundry soap
    Glue

Directions:

Draw several stems with a brown crayon onto the piece of blue paper. Small green leaves can also be added.

Mix one part white powdered tempera, one part powdered laundry detergent, and two parts water. Dip an index finger into the paint mixture. Use this finger to print small circles along the stems. A small bow of yarn or ribbon can be glued near the bottom of the stems.

Blossoming Tree

Ages: 6-10
Materials:
    Light blue construction paper
    Crayons
    Pink and green tissue paper
    Glue

Directions:

Fringe several layers of tissue paper into $1/16''$-$1/8''$ strips. Then trim across the fringe forming $1/16''$-$1/8''$ squares.

Draw a spring picture which includes a tree without leaves onto the blue paper. Dab small amounts of glue on the branches of the tree and quickly sprinkle with tissue paper. This is best done in a small cardboard box so that the excess tissue can be shaken off and reused with a minimum of mess.

Plastic Butterfly

Ages: 4-10
Materials:
    Transparent disposable plastic glasses (6-12 ounces)
    Broad tip permanent marker
    12″ piece of black chenille wire
    Glue
    Ice pick or darning needle
    Thread
    Aluminum foil

Directions:

Draw a design on the outside of the cup with the markers. Preheat oven to 350°. Cover a cookie tray with aluminum foil. Place inverted cup on cookie tray and put in oven. Watch carefully because baking time varies. Remove quickly as the cup begins to melt and flatten. Cool. Heat the metal tip of an ice pick or darning needle. While still hot, melt a small hole for inserting a thread hanger by gently pressing the hot tip through the plastic.

Make the butterfly's body from the chenille wire by first folding the wire in half. Starting at the folded end wrap all but the last inch around a pencil. Pull the two ends apart to form antennae. Glue the body onto the wings. Push an 8″ piece of thread through the hole and tie ends together.

Paper Butterfly

Ages: 5-10
Materials:
    Construction paper: black, green, and yellow
    Yarn or string
    Stapler
    Glue

Directions:

Cut one black and two green 1″ x 12″ strips. Cut two 1″ x 9″ yellow strips. Fold the black strip in half. If you wish to hang the butterfly, lay a 24″ piece of yarn down the middle of the black strip. Place a green strip above and below the black strip. Next, place a yellow strip above and below the green strips. Center the strips over the black strip. Staple all five strips and yarn together in the center. First curl, fold, bend, or glue both yellow strips in a similar fashion. Next curl, fold, bend, or glue both green strips in a similar fashion. (Both sides should look alike so that a symmetrical design is produced.) Curl the two open ends of the black strip for antennae.

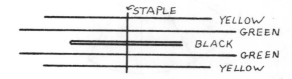

Banners

Ages: 7-10
Materials:
- Construction paper
- Waxed paper
- Glue
- Iron
- Newsprint
- Yarn
- Paper punch

Directions:

Cut waxed paper into a piece 18″ long. Fold in half. Cut various summer motifs from construction paper (sun, flowers, butterflies, insects). Arrange shapes between the two layers of waxed paper. Heat iron on a warm setting. Place a sheet of newsprint over the waxed paper and iron the design. Fold a 9″ x 2″ strip of paper in half. Slide the waxed paper into the folded strip and glue in place. Punch a hole at each end of the strip and thread a 36″ piece of yarn through the holes for the hanger. Tie ends of yarn in a single knot.

Leaf Rubbings

Ages: 8-10
Materials:
- Tissue paper: autumn colors
- White construction paper
- White glue
- Large brush or small sponge
- Leaves
- Crayons

Directions:

Place a leaf, vein side up, under a piece of tissue paper. Rub over the tissue with the side of a black or dark brown crayon. Cut out the leaf shape. Continue making additional rubbings. Make a diluted glue solution by mixing one part glue and three parts water. Paint entire surface of the white paper with the glue. Quickly arrange the tissue leaves on the paper. Give the entire paper another light coat of diluted glue. After the paint dries, crayon accents (tree, branches) can be added.
Variation:

Use at least two shades of blue tissue paper to cut snowflakes of varying sizes. Mount on white construction paper following the above directions.

Burlap Flowers

Ages: 5-7
Materials:
- Construction paper
- Burlap
- White glue
- Yellow food coloring
- Crayons
- Waxed paper

Directions:

Cut burlap into 1½″ squares following the grain of the fabric as you cut. Paint a small circle—about the size of a dime—of white glue which has been tinted with yellow food coloring in the center of each square. Place the burlap on waxed paper while the glue dries. Allow time for the glue to dry completely.

Fringe all four sides of each square until the glued center is reached producing an "X"-shaped flower. Glue the flower onto a piece of construction paper and use crayons to draw leaves, stems, etc.

Sunbleached Designs

Ages: 7-10
Materials:
- Dark construction paper
- Masking tape

Directions:

Cut from construction paper designs, objects, or letters. Arrange on a sheet of dark paper. Roll small pieces of masking tape into tubes. Place under the cut-out shapes and attach them to the sheet of dark paper. Tape the picture to a sunny window—design side out. Leave at the window at least two days. Remove from the window. Carefully peel off the shapes. The picture should be visible on the paper because the sun has bleached the exposed areas of the paper.

Painted Autumn Leaves

Ages: 8-10
Materials:
    Leaves
    Paint brushes
    Tempera
    Construction paper
    Newsprint

Directions:

Lay a leaf, vein side up, on a piece of newsprint. Paint the leaf with tempera. Place the leaf on a clean sheet of newsprint. Place a sheet of construction paper on top of the leaf and rub gently. Lift the paper carefully off the leaf. Additional prints may be made on the same paper.
Variation:
Substitute bleach for tempera and use a bright or dark shade of construction paper. Follow the above directions.

Waxed Leaves

Ages: 8-10
Materials:
    Leaves
    Crayons
    Drawing paper
    Iron
    Newsprint

Directions:

Gather fresh green leaves which are heavily veined. Color the veined side of several leaves with autumn colors. Use light strokes of the crayon coloring from the center to the edge of the leaf. Place one leaf at a time, crayoned side up, on a folded section of newsprint. Cover the leaf with a piece of drawing paper and press with a warm iron. Lift the iron up and down rather than sliding back and forth. Carefully peel paper from leaves.

Apple Basket

Ages: 5-8
Materials:
    Apple
    Red food coloring
    Drawing paper
    Construction paper: green, brown
    Plate
    Glue

Directions:

Slice an apple in half through the stem. Add red food coloring to two tablespoons of water. Dip the apple into the red solution and then firmly press the apple onto a piece of drawing paper. Continue to print apples as they might be found in a bushel basket. From construction paper cut stems, leaves, and a basket. Glue pieces into place.

Autumn Scene

Ages: 7-10
Materials:
    Drawing paper
    Crayons
    Crayon shavings *(Use autumn colors and make shavings by sharpening crayons with a hand held pencil sharpener.)*
    Waxed paper
    Iron
    Newsprint

Directions:

Draw an autumn scene which includes a tree without leaves. When the picture is complete sprinkle some crayon shavings on the branches of the tree and on the ground under the tree. Cover the picture with waxed paper and then a sheet of newsprint. Iron with a warm iron. Quickly remove both the newsprint and the waxed paper.

Three-dimensional Snowman

Ages: 6-8
Materials:
    Construction paper
    Glue
    Yarn and assorted trims

Directions:

Cut a 12" x 4" and a 9" x 3" strip of white construction paper. Overlap the short ends of each strip forming two tubes and glue ends together. Staple the two rolled strips together. Glue the resulting snowman onto a sheet of blue paper. Use construction paper, yarn, and assorted trims to complete snowman.

Pinecone Bird Feeder

Ages: 4-7
Materials:
  Pinecone
  Yarn or string
  Solid shortening
  Dry cereal
  Waxed paper
  Plastic sandwich bag

Directions:

Tie a piece of yarn securely around the pointed end of a pinecone. Allow enough extra yarn so that later the pinecone can be tied onto a tree. Place a tablespoon of solid shortening on a small piece of waxed paper. Pick up a piece of cereal, scoop a small amount of shortening onto it, and then place the cereal onto a pinecone petal with the shortening side down. The shortening will act as a glue holding the cereal in place. Place pinecone in the plastic bag to take feeder home.

Snowman

Ages: 5-10
Materials:
  Construction paper
  Brush
  Diluted glue *(2 parts water to 1 part glue)*
  "Snow" *(equal parts of flour and salt)*
  Crayons

Directions:

Paint a snowman shape with the diluted glue on a piece of blue construction paper. Small drops of glue can be printed on the paper with the eraser end of a pencil. Quickly dust entire paper with the flour and salt mixture. Shake off excess. Use various colors of construction paper and/or crayons to add details to the snowman.

Snowflake

Ages: 9-12
Materials:
  12" x 18" sheet of newsprint
  String
  Glue
  Paper punch

Directions:

Cut the newsprint in half making two 6" x 18" pieces. Glue the two pieces together by slightly overlapping the 6" sides. Fold this strip back and forth (accordion style) making each folded section about 1" wide. Punch a hole near one end of the folded strip. *(If the punch will not cut through all the folded paper at once, punch through portions at a time being sure that the holes align.)* Make a slanted cut across the other end. Cut shapes into each folded side. Thread the string through the punched holes. Pull the thread tightly enough that the strip draws itself into a circular shape. Tie the string. Glue the two ends of the strip together.

Snowflake Bookmark

Ages: 7-10
Materials:
  2½" x 6" piece of white construction paper
  2" x 5½" piece of bright blue tissue paper
  Diluted white glue *(1 part glue to 3 parts water)*
  Brush

Directions:

Fold the tissue paper in half producing two 1" x 5½" sections. Then fold the paper in half twice in the other direction so that a 1" x 1⅓" folded pack is produced. Cut shapes into all four sides. Unfold tissue. Paint the entire surface of the white paper with diluted glue. Carefully position tissue on the center of the construction paper. Paint over tissue with another light coat of diluted glue. Let dry.

Robe

Ages: 7-9
Materials:
    Drawing paper
    Construction paper
    Crayons
    Glue

Directions:
Fold an 8" x 9" piece of paper in half. Using pattern 54A trace and then cut out a robe from the folded construction paper. Keeping the robe folded, cut five wavy lines through the fold to within ⅓" of the edge of the robe *(see illustration)*. Unfold robe. Weave three ¾" x 4" strips of contrasting colored paper into the slits of the robe. Adjust strips so that the bottom of the strips are even with the bottom of the robe. Glue the robe on a piece of drawing paper. Use crayons to draw a person (head, neck, feet, and hands) dressed in the robe.

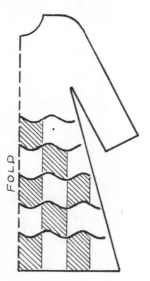

Wave Bottle

Ages: 4-7
Materials:
    Clear plastic bottle with screw-on lid *(shampoo bottle)*
    Blue food coloring
    Liquid vegetable oil
    Glue

Directions:
Fill bottle half full with water. Tint blue with food coloring. Fill to the very top with vegetable oil. Spread a small amount of glue inside the lid of the bottle and screw the lid on tightly.
Hold the bottle on its side and gently rock the bottle's ends up and down slowly. The rocking motion will produce waves in the blue liquid of the bottle. Use for illustrating any story of Jesus on the Sea of Galilee.

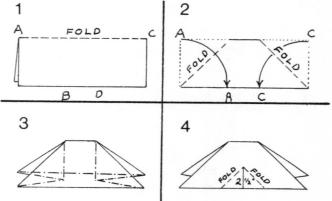

Tent

Ages: 5-9
Materials:
    Drawing paper
    Crayons

Directions:
Fold a 9" x 12" piece of drawing paper following the illustration.
1. Fold the paper in half producing two 4½" x 12" sections.
2. With the paper still folded, fold the top corner A *(folded edge)* down to the bottom *(open edge)* of the paper at B. Bring corner C to D.
3. Open up the paper. Reverse the center folds on each side so that they fold into the center. Reverse one of the diagonal folds on each side so that all folds come toward the center of the paper.
4. Into the center of the front cut a 2½" slit. Fold up each side section along the dotted lines in the diagram to form a door for the tent.
Use crayons to decorate the outside of the tent. People and furnishings could also be drawn inside the front flap.

Trumpet

Ages: 5-9
Materials:
   Brown construction paper
   Drinking straw
   Cellophane tape

Directions:

Cut a horn-shaped trumpet from a 9″ x 12″ piece of paper. Flatten one end of a plastic straw. With your fingernails crease both sides of the flattened end. With scissors notch both sides of the flattened end *(see illustration)*. Tape the straw to the back of the trumpet so that the flattened end extends beyond the mouth end of the trumpet. Put straw into your mouth, hold between your lips, and blow through the straw very forcefully. Press the sides of the straw together with your lips but do not bite the straw with your teeth as you blow.

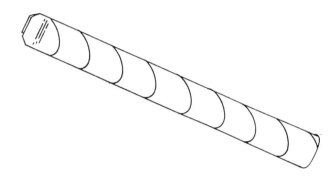

Ring

Ages: 4-7
Materials:
   Pull tab rings from soft drink cans
   Hammer
   Pliers
   Glue
   Glitter
   Waxed paper

Directions:

Remove the pull tabs from the rings with pliers. Lay the ring on a hard surface and hammer the area where the tab was connected to the ring. Check to be sure that any sharp edges have been flattened. Spread glue on both sides of the section where the tab was removed. Dip the glued area into glitter. Let dry on waxed paper.

Use to illustrate Bible stories of various kings, the rich young man, and the prodigal son.

Parting the Water

Ages: 5-8
Materials:
   Construction paper: light blue, dark blue, brown
   Glue
   Crayons

Directions:

Glue a 1½″ x 12″ strip of brown paper across one long edge of the 9″ x 12″ piece of light blue paper. Using pattern 51A, cut two water pieces from the dark blue paper. Glue the outside, short, straight edge of a water piece to the 9″ x 12″ sheet leaving the center free. Position the river pieces so that they cover the brown strip. Fold the river pieces up diagonally so that the bottom edge lies along the 9″ edge of the light blue paper. Use crayons to illustrate the characters of the story.
Character suggestions:
1. Moses crossing the Red Sea
2. God's people crossing into the Promised Land through the River Jordan
3. Elisha striking the water with Elijah's cloak

Shield

Ages: 4-7
Materials:
   9″ paper plate
   Crayons
   White poster board
   Stapler

Directions:

Decorate the back of the plate with crayons. Cut a 1″ x 7½″ piece of poster board. Lay across diameter of undecorated side of plate. Staple to the rim of the plate on both sides. This is the carrying handle.

Diorama

Ages: 7-10
Materials:
   Construction paper
   Glue

Directions:

Fold a 9″ x 12″ piece of light blue paper in half producing two 6″ x 9″ sections. Cut a 4″ x 12″ and a 2″ x 9″ strip from green, blue, or brown paper. Fold strips in half and then fold back a one-inch tab on the end of each strip. If desired scallop the top edge of the blue strip to look like water. Place folded 4″ x 12″ strip inside the folded 9″ x 12″ blue paper. Line up edges and glue tabs to the back of the 9″ x 12″ piece. Place 2″ x 9″ folded strip inside 4″ x 12″ piece, line up edges, and glue tabs to outside. Use assorted construction paper to depict people and objects in Bible story.

Basket

Ages: 4-7
Materials:
   Construction paper

Directions:

Fold a 6″ x 12″ piece of paper in half producing two 6″ x 6″ sections. Using pattern 51B, trace and cut out the basket. Also cut a 5″ x 3″ piece of paper. Fold the paper in half producing two 5″ x 1½″ sections and slip this paper into the V-shaped notch of the basket. Pull the basket pieces away from each other so that only a ½″ portion of the V-shaped piece extends beyond the basket.

Prison Crayon Rubbing

Ages: 6-11
Materials:
   Lightweight drawing paper
   Corrugated cardboard
   Crayons
   Tape

Directions:

Remove the top layer of paper from the sheet of cardboard. The cardboard piece should be slightly larger than the drawing paper which will be used.

Using crayons, draw a picture of Paul in prison. Then, place picture on the cardboard. Tape corners of the paper to the cardboard. Remove the paper from a black crayon. Using the sides of the crayon rub over the entire picture.

Character suggestions:
1. Noah's ark *(use blue crayon)*
2. Rain after the drought (Elijah)

Rocking Boat

Ages: 4-7
Materials:
   9″ paper plate
   Construction paper
   Crayons
   Glue
   Stapler

Directions:

Color the bottom of the plate blue. If desired, details such as fish, nets, and waves can be added. Fold the paper plate in half, colored side out. Cut scalloped waves across the center of the folded area leaving one inch of the fold uncut at each end. From construction paper cut a sail and a boat. Glue boat pieces together. Slide the bottom ½″ of the boat between the waves cut on the plate. Center the boat on the plate and staple to secure. Pull the bottom ridges of the plate apart slightly so that the plate will stand up. Tap one side of the plate gently to rock the boat on the waves.

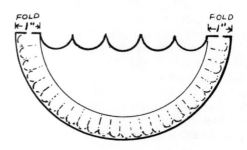

Noah's Rainbow

Ages: 3-6
Materials:

Construction paper: four different colors
Stapler

Directions:

Using the four different colors, cut paper into one 1" x 12" strip, one 1" x 11" strip, one 1" x 10" strip, and one 1" x 9" strip. Lay the strips on top of each other starting with the longest and ending with the shortest. Place all 1" ends on one side together and staple close to the edge. Place 1" ends of other side together and staple close to the edge. Rainbow can stand on its ends.

Ladder

Ages: 6-9
Materials:

Lightweight paper (typing paper, newsprint, or newspaper)

Directions:

Starting at a short side of the paper, roll entire paper into a tube about 1" in diameter. Flatten tube. Cut out a rectangular shape from one side of the tube *(see illustration)*. Carefully unroll.

CUT AWAY

Palm Tree

Ages: 4-7
Materials:

12" x 18" piece newsprint
Crayons: brown, green
Glue

Directions:

With a pencil, mark paper as indicated in illustration. Also, mark the top 4" on the back side of the paper. Color both top sections green and the bottom side section brown. Fold the paper in half three times producing a 2¼" x 12" section. Using pattern 52B, cut a palm leaf shape from the green section. Unfold. Place paper on table with brown area face down. Beginning with the short side opposite the brown section, roll the paper into a tube about 1" in diameter. Glue end along the brown trunk to secure.

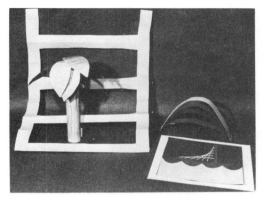

String Design Boat

Ages: 6-8
Materials:

Blue poster board
White string, yarn, or crochet thread
Construction paper: blue, brown
Glue
Cellophane tape
Tapestry needle

Directions:

Cut poster board into 7" x 7" piece. Mark two 3" lines onto the paper as indicated in illustration. Mark each 3" line into ½" sections. Use a tapestry needle to make a hole at each of these ½" points. Starting at the top of the vertical line, number the ½" points from one to six. Starting at the end where the two lines meet, number the ½" points from one to six along the vertical line. Thread a 36" piece of string into a tapestry needle and tape the end of the string to the poster board near the horizontal hole marked 1. Push the needle and thread through 1 on the horizontal line and bring it back through 1 of the vertical line. Thread needle through 2 of the vertical line and bring it back through 2 of the horizontal line. Take it through 3 of the horizontal line and bring it back through 3 of the vertical line. Continue in a similar manner until both number 6 holes are connected with thread. Trim off excess thread. Tape thread end to back of paper. The string design is a sail. From construction paper cut a mast, boat, and water. Glue pieces into place.

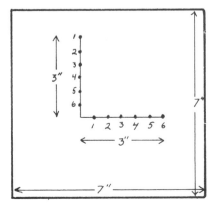

Night Picture

Ages: 5-9
Materials:
    Black construction paper
    Crayons
    Optional: orange tempera paint

Directions:
Draw picture depicting a night scene in the Bible story with crayons on the black paper. If fire was part of the story, use tempera paint to add the fire accents.
Character suggestions:
1. Nicodemus and Jesus
2. Pillar of fire at night
3. Joshua and his soldiers with their pitchers and torches

Church Montage

Ages: 5-9
Materials:
    Drawing paper
    Magazines
    Glue

Directions:
Draw the outline of a church building on a 9" x 12" piece of drawing paper. Turn the paper over so that the outline of the church building is face down. Cut pictures of people from the magazines. Glue these pictures on the 9" x 12" paper until the paper is completely covered. Turn the paper over and cut out the church shape.

Paper Plate Puppet

Ages: 4-7
Materials:
  9" paper plate
  Masking or strapping tape
  Crayons

Directions:
  Cut a slit in the plate as indicated in the illustration. This is the mouth. Color over the slit with a red crayon being sure that the color reaches about 1/8" above and below the slit. Use crayons to draw a nose, eyes, and any other facial details desired. On the back of the plate at each end of the slit place a 1" piece of tape. This will help prevent the plate from tearing.
  To make the puppet talk, pull up on the top half and down on the bottom half of the plate.

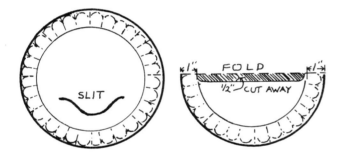

Talking Plate Puppet

Ages: 5-7
Materials:
  Two 9" paper plates
  Crayons or markers
  Glue
  Red construction paper

Directions:
  Fold one plate in half and cut a notch 1/2" wide along the center fold. *(See illustration.)* Glue the notched plate on top of another plate gluing only the rim. Let the glue dry.
  Use crayons to draw the front of the head on one half of the notched plate and the back of the head on the other half of the notched plate. Glue a red paper circle in the center of the unnotched plate for the mouth.
  To make the puppet talk, slip fingers into the top pocket and the thumb into the bottom pocket. Then move the fingers and thumb up and down.

Paper Tube Puppet

Ages: 6-8
Materials:
  9" x 12" piece of drawing paper
  Crayons
  Glue
  Stapler

Directions:
  Roll the drawing paper into a 12" tube overlapping the edges 1". Hold the tube in place with several staples. Place a small amount of glue in the top of the tube. Flatten the top half of the tube and hold until the glue sets. Use scissors to round off the top two corners. Use crayons to draw a puppet representing a Biblical character or a self portrait.

Envelope Puppet

Ages: 3-5
Materials:
  Standard sized white envelope
  Crayons
  Yarn cut into 1½" pieces

Directions:
  Seal the envelope shut. Cut the envelope open by slicing off ½" from one of the short sides. With the open end being the bottom, draw a face on the envelope. Glue small pieces of yarn around the sides and top of the envelope for hair. Slip the envelope onto four fingers and make it move.

Paper Bag Puppets

Ages: 6-8
Materials:
Drawing paper
Paper lunch bags
Crayons
Glue

Directions:

Talking bag: Cut a 5″ x 10″ piece of drawing paper and fold it in half producing two 5″ x 5″ sections. With scissors round off the corners of the drawing paper. Glue the paper onto the bag so that the fold lies along the bottom flap of the bag. Glue half of the paper to the bottom of the bag allowing part of the paper to extend beyond the bag. Glue the other half of the paper into the flap and return bag to its original folded position.

Use crayons to draw a face. The entire face except the lower lip and chin should be on the upper half of the drawing paper. Draw the lower lip on the bottom half of the paper. Clothes details can be drawn on the bag.

To make the puppet talk, place fingers in the flap of the bag and then move the fingers up and down.

Blinking bag: Draw closed eyes on the bottom of the bag, while the bag is folded, extending the bottom of the lid and lashes onto the bag's front. Lift the flap and draw the rest of the open eye under the flap. Complete the face (both on top and underneath flap).

To make the puppet open and shut its eyes, place four fingers into the flap of the bag and move fingers up and down.

Animal Headbands

Ages: 4-6
Materials:
Construction paper: white for sheep; brown, gray, or black for donkey; brown for cattle
Glue
Stapler

Directions:

Staple the short ends of two 2″ x 18″ strips together. Decorate the strips as follows:

Sheep: cut a topknot of wool by scalloping the edges of a 5½″ x 3½″ piece of white paper. Cut ears from 3″ x 2″ pieces of white paper and pink centers for the ears from 2″ x 1″ pieces of paper.

Donkey: cut a mane from a 6″ x 4½″ piece of paper of a contrasting color; ears from 2½″ x 6″ pieces; center for the ears from 4½″ x 1½″ pieces of pink paper.

Cow: cut ears from 2″ x 3″ pieces; centers for the ears from 1″ x 2″ pieces of pink paper; horns from 3″ x 3″ pieces of yellow paper; topknot from 6″ x 4½″ piece.

Fit the strip around the child's head, trim away excess paper from strip, overlap ends, and staple.

Armor

Ages: 4-7
Materials:
Large grocery bag
Crayons

Directions:

With the bag folded shut, round off the corners of the open end of the bag. Cut away the side sections leaving a 2½″ band which is 7½″ from the closed bottom of the bag. This will create armholes for the armor.

Cut a neck hole from the bottom of the bag leaving 2½″ bands on each side for the shoulders. Cut across the front and back, curving slightly into the front and back of the bag. Decorate with crayons.

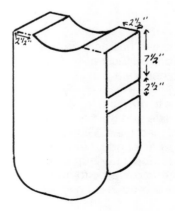

Finger Puppet

Ages: 4-6
Materials:
Felt: brown, gold, white, or gray
Fine-point non-permanent marker or black ball-point pen

Directions:
Using pattern 52D, cut hair and beard for puppet from felt. Slip index finger through the two slits in the felt so that the center felt section covers the nail. The puppet should fit snuggly so that it stays in place. Since the size of children's fingers vary greatly, the center slit might need to be lengthened to slip the puppet onto the finger of a child with larger hands. To complete the puppet, use the marker or pen to draw eyes and a nose onto the index finger.

Bandage Puppet

Ages: 3-6
Materials:
Bandage—3/4" wide
Fine-point permanent marker

Directions:
Wrap the bandage around index finger. Use marker to draw face on padded center of bandage.

Peanut Puppet

Ages: 3-6
Materials:
Peanuts in the shell
Knife
Fine-tip permanent marker

Directions:
Cut shells in half with knife and remove peanuts. Draw faces onto the peanut shells with the marker. Place the shells onto the fingertips.

Animal Bag Puppet

Ages: 5-7
Materials:
Paper lunch bag
Construction paper
Glue
Crayons

Directions:
Cut a piece of red paper as wide as the bag's front and 2" high. Glue this piece on the front of the bag *(the side on which the bag's bottom rests when the bag is folded shut)* so that one side rests along the bottom of the bag. Fold the bag bottom back over the red paper. This area will become the mouth. From construction paper, or with crayons, make the animal's head on the bottom of the bag. Also from construction paper cut the front legs and glue them onto the sides of the bag. To make the animal open its mouth, place four fingers into the bottom of the bag. Move the fingers up and down moving the mouth.

Tissue Lamb

Ages: 4-7
Materials:
Two white tissues
Small rubber band
Cotton ball
Construction paper: white and black
Pink crayon
Glue
Paper punch

Directions:
Form one tissue into a tight ball. Place the tissue ball in the center of the second tissue. Gather the tissue around the ball and wrap the rubber band tightly around the tissue and the ball inside. Using a paper punch, cut two black eyes from paper. Also cut ears from the white paper and color the centers pink. Glue eyes, ears, and a small section of a cotton ball (forelock) in place to complete the puppet.

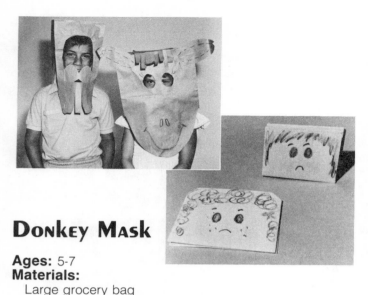

Donkey Mask

Ages: 5-7
Materials:
    Large grocery bag
    Crayons
    Glue

Directions:

Cut the bag as indicated in illustration. Put the bag on the child's head and mark the bag where the eyes should appear. Remove the bag from the child's head and cut large eye openings. Cut ears and a mane from the scraps. Glue ears and mane in place. Fold mane over the top of face, and fringe. Use crayons to add nostrils, mouth, eye lashes, ear details, etc.

Wigs

Ages: 5-7
Materials:
    20-pound paper bag with a flat bottom measuring approximately 8½" x 6" x 14"
    Yellow construction paper

Directions:

Woman's wig: cut the bag as illustrated in the photo. Fringe the bottom half of the bag and curl the hair by rolling the paper strips produced tightly around a pencil.

Man's wig: cut out the face opening as illustrated in the photo. Fringe the bottom half of the sides and back of bag. Also fringe beard to within 2" of the face opening. If desired, curl hair and beard. Cut a mustache from another bag and glue it to the bag at the base of the face opening.

If the Biblical character being dramatized is a king or queen, a crown can be cut from construction paper and stapled into place.

Talking Envelope Puppet

Ages: 6-8
Materials:
    Standard sized white envelope
    Crayons

Directions:

Seal the envelope shut. Fold the envelope in half with the seal folded to the inside. Notch both corners of the fold and cut across the top layer only of the fold. *(The sealed side of the envelope will remain uncut and two pockets will be created.)* With crayons draw the front of the head on one side of the outside and the back of the head on the other side. The openings of the pockets should be at the top of the head. Color the inside fold of the envelope as a mouth. To make the puppet talk, slip four fingers into the top pocket and the thumb into the bottom pocket. Move the four fingers up and down to make the mouth open and close.

Talking Fold-up Puppet

Ages: 7-9
Materials:
    9" x 12" piece of drawing paper
    Crayons
    Glue

Directions:

1. Fold paper in half (9" x 6").
2. Fold paper in half again (9" x 3").
3. Fold paper in half in the opposite directions.
4. Fold each section in half by bringing up each open end to the outside fold. Glue so these two sections remain folded.

Use crayons to color the inside red (mouth), one outside section as the face excluding the mouth, and the other outside section as the back of the head. To make the puppet talk, slip the thumb into the lower pocket and 3 or 4 fingers into the upper pocket. Move fingers and thumb up and down.

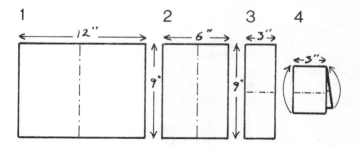

Robes

Ages: 4-7
Materials:
   Large grocery bag
   Crayons

Directions:

Cut bag's front in half beginning at the center of the open end and cutting to the bag's bottom. Continue cutting into the bag's bottom 1½″. Cut away a large oval from the bag's bottom for a neck opening. Cut an oval in both side sections 2″ from the bag's bottom for arm openings. Decorate with crayons.
Character suggestions:
1. Joseph and his coat of many colors.
2. Samuel and the coat his mother made him each year.
3. The prodigal son and the robe his father gave him on his return.
4. Dorcas and the robes she made for the needy.

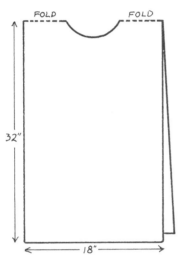

Cloth Costumes

Ages: 5-8
Materials:
   Polyester doubleknits or fabrics that will not fray when cut

Directions:

Robe: cut robes from a single piece of fabric folded as indicated in illustration. Note the fold at the shoulders. Leave sides open. No sewing is required.
   Headdress: cut a 24″ square of fabric.
   Band for headdress: cut a 1½″ x 36″ strip of fabric.
   Belt: cut a 48″ x 3″ strip of fabric.
   Slip the robe over child's head. Tie the belt around his waist. Center the headdress on the child's head with the front falling over the child's forehead and the remainder covering the back of his head. Tie band around his head to secure headdress.
   Make several costumes and keep them in your classroom as part of a permanent collection of aids for dramatization of Bible stories.

Bible Story Pop-up Cup

Ages: 3-6
Materials:
   Styrofoam Cup
   Small pictures
   Cellophane tape
   Straws

Directions:

Make three to four holes in the bottom of the cup which are large enough to allow a straw to move through freely. Tape each straw to the back of a small picture. Place the straw into the cup and through the hole in the cup's bottom. Depending on the size of the pictures, three or four pictures and straws should be able to fit in the cup. As the story is told, raise the picture being discussed out of the cup so the picture will be visible to the children.

Magnetic Picture

Ages: 4-7
Materials:
   Tagboard or poster board
   Pictures from lesson visual aids
   Cellophane tape
   Small disc-shaped magnets
   Glue

Directions:

If a background picture from the visual aids is to be used, glue it to a piece of tagboard which is slightly larger than the picture. Tape paper clips to the back of the smaller pictures. Lay the pictures on the tagboard. Place a magnet under the tagboard directly behind each picture. As the story is being told, hold up the tagboard and move the pictures by moving the magnets behind the tagboard.

King David

Ages: 4-8
Materials:
   Drawing Paper
   Crayons
   Stapler

Directions:

Trace crown and face onto a 9″ x 12″ paper as indicated in the illustration. Cut at top edge producing a crown shape. Using crayons, color details for the face, crown, and beard. Color the bottom half of the back of the paper the same color as the beard. Cut fringes into the bottom half of the paper. Curl each strip of fringe by rolling it tightly around a pencil. Roll the head into a tube shape. Overlap the back top edges slightly, then staple to secure.

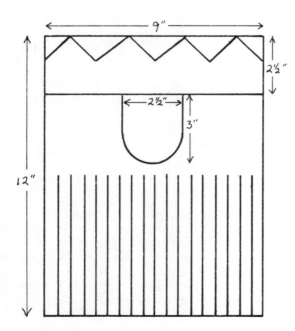

Twirling Prison Pictures

Ages: 6-10
Materials:
   Drawing paper
   Plastic drinking straw
   Cellophane tape
   Crayons

Directions:

Cut the drawing paper into 4½″ x 4½″ squares. On one paper draw the bars of a prison. On the other paper draw a Biblical character who was placed in prison (Joseph, Paul, John the Baptist). Glue these two pieces together back-to-back. Cut two 1″ slots in the top of a straw. *(See illustration.)* Slide the paper into the slot. Tape the straw sections on the front and back of the paper. To create the illusion of a person in prison, revolve the straw back and forth quickly between your palms.
Variation:
Draw Jonah and put him in the big fish. Follow the same directions except on one paper draw a big fish and on the other draw Jonah.

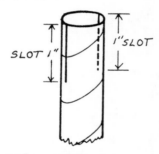

Samson Planter

Ages: 4-7
Materials:
   12-ounce frozen juice can
   Drawing paper
   Glue
   Crayons
   Soil
   Seeds *(Alfalfa, radish, or clover seeds are all sold at any health food store and work well in that they are inexpensive and sprout in about two days.)*

Directions:

Cut a piece of drawing paper so that it will fit around the outside of a juice can. In the center third of the drawing paper draw Samson's face. Fill the rest of the paper with Samson's hair. Carefully fill the can to within ½″ of the top with moist soil. Sprinkle a teaspoon of seeds on the soil, cover with a thin layer of additional soil, and water. Glue the picture of Samson around the can. Place in a sunny window. Remind children to water the soil so that Samson's "hair" will grow.

Isaac

Ages: 4-8
Materials:
  Drawing paper
  Crayons
  Stapler

Directions:

Prepare a 9″ x 12″ piece of drawing paper as indicated in the illustration, tracing pattern 52E onto the center edge of one of the 12″ sides. Cut out the traced pattern section. The portion of paper from which the pattern section has been removed represents the hair. Color this section below the fold line only and fringe to within ½″ of the fold. Fold paper and draw the face features in the open area. Roll into a tube shape and staple overlapping ends.

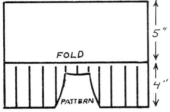

Rebekah with a Pitcher

Ages: 6-10
Materials:
  9″ paper plate
  Construction paper
  Crayons
  Stapler

Directions:

Cut paper plate as indicated in the illustration. Using crayons draw the details of the person's face and clothing. Both the front and back of the arm sections should be colored. From construction paper cut the object to be held in the hands. To complete, bend each side of the bottom section (the skirt) around to the back, overlap slightly, and staple to secure. Next, bend the arm sections around to the front, place the pitcher between the two hands, and staple to secure.
Other character suggestions:
1. Moses holding his rod
2. David holding Saul's spear and jug
3. Mary with a jar of perfume to anoint Jesus
4. Esau with bow and arrow
5. Josiah with a scroll

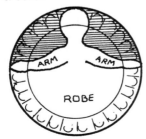

Abraham

Ages: 4-8
Materials:
  Construction paper: black, brown, or gray
  Drawing paper
  Crayons
  Glue
  Stapler

Directions:

Cut a 9″ x 12″ piece of construction paper as indicated in the illustration. Glue a piece of drawing paper behind the center opening. With crayons and scraps from the 9″ x 12″ paper, cut from paper and/or draw facial features and mustache. If desired, fringe and curl beard. When face is complete, roll sheet into tube and staple to secure.

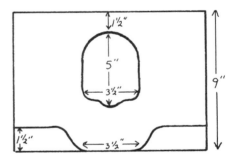

Sarah

Ages: 4-8
Materials:
  Drawing Paper
  Crayons
  Stapler

Directions:

Using a 9″ x 12″ piece of drawing paper, trace pattern 52C onto the center edge of one of the 12″ sides. Cut away this section. If desired, draw an oval shape to define the face area. Color face features and hair. The hair should fill the entire area not covered by the face. Roll into a tube shape, overlap the back edges, and staple to secure. Fringe and curl the hair if desired.

Barabbas Three-dimensional Face

Ages: 6-11
Materials:
　Drawing paper
　Crayons
　Glue

Directions:
　Fold a 9" x 12" piece of drawing paper in half producing two 4½" x 12" sections. Place pattern 52A along fold and trace heavy lines. Cut along the traced lines. Fold center section (nose) as indicated by the dotted lines on the pattern. Glue this face onto another 9" x 12" piece of drawing paper, overlapping the top and bottom sections about ½". This will cause the nose section to protrude. Use crayons to complete details of the face.

Widow of Nain Portrait

Ages: 4-8
Materials:
　9" paper plate
　White construction paper
　Glue
　Crayons

Directions:
　Cut plate in desired shape for man, woman, or child. *(See "Family Portraits".)* Cut a center circle from another paper plate. Fold this circle in half and cut ½" above the fold. This will be your pattern. Trace and cut out a semicircle from white paper. Crease the semicircle ½" from straight edge and glue the creased tab across the center section of the plate. Hold the white semicircle down and draw a happy face. Next, fold the semicircle up and draw a sad face. Use these faces to represent someone, like the Widow of Nain, whose sadness was turned into joy because of God's love and care.

Moses and the Stone Tablets

Ages: 6-10
Materials:
　Drawing paper
　Construction paper
　Crayons
　Stapler

Directions:
　Fold a 6" x 18" piece of drawing paper in half producing two 6" x 9" sections. Trace pattern 53A onto this paper. Cut out shape and unfold. Use crayons to color the front of the face and both sides of the outstretched arms. Cut stone tablets from construction paper. Place the tablets on one hand and staple the other hand on top.
Character suggestions:
1. Noah with a dove.
2. Gideon's soldier with a trumpet
3. Sarah holding baby Isaac
4. A Wise-man with a gift

Naaman Mobile

Ages: 6-10
Materials:
　Construction paper
　Drawing paper
　Thread
　Glue
　Crayons
　Cellophane tape

Directions:
　Using construction paper and pattern 54A, trace and cut two robes. Trace and cut two heads from drawing paper using pattern 54B. Provide additional drawing paper from which hands can be cut. On one head draw a happy face and on the other a sad face. Glue hands onto the robe. Center one head, colored side down, ¼" above the robe. Lay a 24" thread along the center of the head and robe so that one end of the thread touches the bottom of the robe and the excess thread extends above the head. Tape thread into place. Glue the second head, colored side up, over the first head, and glue. Glue second robe on top of the first with the thread in between so it is hidden. This mobile shows Naaman's face before and after he was healed.
Character suggestions:
1. Mary or Martha before and after the resurrection of Lazarus.
2. A disciple before and after the resurrection of Christ.

Moses Stocking Head

Ages: 8-11
Materials:
Lightweight metal clothes hanger
Panty hose *(use a leg section which has no runs or holes)*
Construction paper
Glue
Thread

Directions:
Bend a hanger into a head *(full face or profile)* shape. Slip the hanger into a leg from the panty hose. Push the hanger in as far as it will go stretching the toe section around the bottom of the hanger. Tie the panty hose to the top of the hanger with thread. Trim away excess panty hose. Use construction paper to make face features, hair, beard, etc. Glue these in place onto the face.

Paul and Friends

Ages: 6-10
Materials:
Paper bags (any size bag with a flat bottom will work)
Crayons
Glue

Directions:
Fold the bag so that it lies flat with the bag's bottom on the underside. Using crayons draw a Bible character. The figure should be as tall as the bag with its feet drawn at the bottom of the bag. When the figure is completely drawn, cut away from the front and back of the bag around the figure. Remove both side sections from the bag. Glue the top third of the front and back sections together. Flatten base so that the figure will stand up.

Prophet Isaiah

Ages: 6-10
Materials:
Construction Paper
Crayons
Glue

Directions:
Fold a 9" x 7" piece of construction paper in half producing two 9" x 3½" sections. Using pattern 60A, trace and cut the robe from this paper. Cut a 4½" x 3" piece of construction paper into a pear shape for the hair and beard. Round the corners of a 2½" x 2" piece of construction paper for the face. First, draw with crayons the features of a face on this piece and then glue the face onto the top part of the beard piece. Slide the face and beard into the two slots of the partially folded robe piece. Cut out hands, and glue to the base of the sleeves.

Family Portraits

Ages: 4-8
Materials:
9" paper plates
Crayons

Directions:
Cut plate as indicated in the illustrations. Use crayons to complete face features, hair, beard, etc. This may be a self portrait or the portrait of anyone in a Bible story.

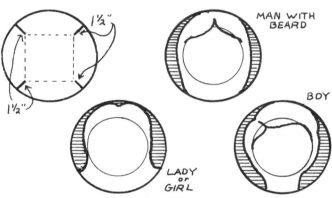

Happy Hannah

Ages: 5-8
Materials:
Drawing paper
Crayons
Stapler
Construction paper

Directions:
Cut a circle with a 9" diameter from drawing paper. Cut 1½" slits into the paper as indicated in the illustration. Use crayons to draw a face in the center of the circle. Crayons can be used to draw hair around the edge of the circle. Fold the paper along the dotted lines shown in the diagram. Overlap paper edges at slits and staple to secure. If desired, hair can be made from 1" strips of construction paper. Glue strips to sides and top of face after it has been stapled. To curl strips roll pieces around a pencil before gluing.

Stand-up Animals

Ages: 4-8
Materials:
  Construction paper: white for lamb, gray for donkey, brown and yellow for cattle
  Crayons
  Glue
  Cotton ball for lamb

Directions:
Fold a 9" x 12" piece of construction paper in half producing two 4½" x 12" sections. For all three animals, trace the lamb's head pattern 53C onto the center of the open 12" edge. Cut out the traced section. Cut a one-inch slit into each end of the fold. Fold back each of the four sections made by the slits.

If making a donkey or a cow, use the donkey and cow pattern 53B to trace and cut a head. Also cut ears and horns (cow) from paper. Glue the ears, horns (cow), and cotton balls (lamb) into place. Use crayons to draw the face. To complete the animal, glue the head onto the folded flaps of the body. You may add tails cut from construction paper to the donkey and cow. A cotton ball would make a tail for the lamb.

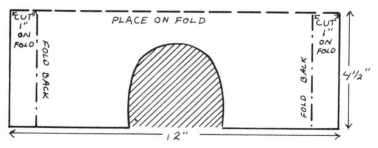

Animal Heads

Ages: 4-8
Materials:
  Construction paper: brown, gray or black for the animal, assorted colors for trim.
  Glue
  Crayons or markers

Directions:
Cut the construction paper into 6" x 18" strips. Fold in half. Open strip, place the head pattern 55A along the fold, trace, and cut out. Cut the neck section as indicated in the illustration keeping the head and neck connected at the fold. Fold head section down. Use crayons and construction paper to add facial features, mane, and ears.
Variation:
For a cow, follow the same directions for basic construction. Add horns and smaller ears for trim.

Paper Bag Animal Head

Ages: 4-8
Materials:
  Paper lunch bag
  Large sheet of newspaper
  Construction paper: pink and gray for donkey; brown, pink, and yellow for cattle
  Crayons
  Glue
  Stapler

Directions:
Draw a mouth on the bottom of the bag. Draw a face on one of the flat sides of the bag. Color the top fourth of the bag on the front and the back for the mane.

Crumple the newspaper and place inside the bag. Shut the bag by folding forward the top fourth of the bag making the mane. To shape the head, fold both corners of the mane to the back and staple to secure. Fringe the mane. Cut ears and horns from construction paper. Glue or staple ears and horns into place.

Cone-shaped Animal Heads

Ages: 4-8
Materials:
 Construction paper: gray, black, or brown
 Crayons
 Stapler

Directions:
 Fold a 9″ x 12″ piece of construction paper in half producing two 9″ x 6″ sections. Lay pattern 57A along the fold, trace, and cut out. With crayons, draw the features of the animal's face. The rectangular section between the ears should be colored on both sides, fringed, and folded forward. (This is its forelock.) If desired, curl fringe by rolling sections around a pencil. Crease ears and fold down. Cut horns from yellow paper and glue onto cattle. Overlap the bottom corners so that a cone shape is produced, and staple to secure.

Animated Animals

Ages: 4-8
Materials:
 Construction paper: green for base; brown, gray, or
    black for animal
 Glue
 Crayons

Directions:
 Cut a 6″ x 9″ piece of green paper for the base. Cut a 4½″ x 12″ piece of paper for the animal's body. Fold paper in half producing two 4½″ x 6″ sections. Use patterns 54C and 55B to trace body and head pieces. Cut out pieces. Glue ends of strip onto the base so that the strip forms an inverted "U" shape and the body stands erect. Decorate head with construction paper and crayon details.

Sheep Planter

Ages: 4-7
Materials:
 Styrofoam egg
 Construction paper: white and black
 Pink crayon
 Two craft sticks
 Cotton ball
 Paper punch
 Glue
 Serrated spoon or knife
 Soil
 Seeds *(Use alfalfa, radish, or clover. These are all sold
    at health food stores and will sprout in about two
    days.)*

Directions:
 Using a serrated spoon or knife, hollow out a cavity in the center of the Styrofoam egg. Cut a 1½″ piece off of each end of two craft sticks making a total of four. Push the craft sticks into the solid bottom of the body to make four legs. Push these sticks in only far enough to secure—do not penetrate the hollowed out area. Use a paper punch to make eyes from black paper. Cut ears from the white paper and color the center with the pink crayon. Glue eyes, ears, and cotton ball into place. Place moist soil into the hollowed out area and sprinkle the top of the soil with seeds. Cover the seeds with soil. Keep moist until the seeds sprout.

Styrofoam Cup Lamb

Age: 4-7
Materials:
 Two Styrofoam cups
 Brass paper fastener
 Construction paper: black and white
 Cotton ball
 Glue

Directions:
 Attach the side of one cup to the bottom of another cup with the brass fastener. Cut ears, eyes, and nose from construction paper. Color the center portion of the ears pink. Glue these pieces in place along with a cotton ball between the ears to complete.

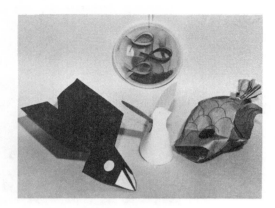

Circular Bird

Ages: 4-7
Materials:
    Construction paper
    Crayons

Directions:
Trace and cut out pattern 61A on construction paper. With crayons, draw one eye and a beak on the front and back of the head. Wrap the wings around to the back, and slide the two slits into each other.

Paper Bag Fish

Ages: 4-9
Materials:
    Paper lunch bag
    Large sheet of newspaper
    Thread
    Construction paper
    Stapler
    Glue
    Crayons

Directions:
First, decorate the bag with crayons. The bottom of the bag will become the mouth. The remainder of the bag will become the body and tail so children need to draw fish scales all over the bag. To shape the mouth, overlap the two adjacent corners of the short side, and staple. Stuff the bag with a crumpled sheet of newspaper. To form the tail, tie the bag shut with the thread. Glue on eyes and fins cut from construction paper.

Flying Bird

Ages: 4-8
Materials:
    Construction paper: 9" x 12"; white (dove), black (raven), brown (quail)
    Construction paper scraps
    Glue
    Stapler

Directions:
Fold the large piece of paper as a paper airplane. *(See illustration. Most second and third graders should be able to do this if you show them how step by step.)* Staple the front (head) section together to secure. Cut and glue one eye and one beak for each side of the head.

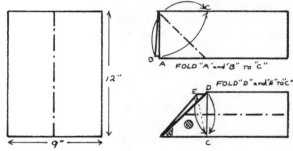

Fish Aquarium

Ages: 4-8
Materials:
    Construction paper
    White glue
    Blue food coloring
    Sand
    String
    Darning needle
    Clear plastic lids at least 6" in diameter *(Lids from soft margarine or frozen dessert topping work well.)*
    Paint brushes or craft sticks

Directions:
With a darning needle make a hole near the rim of the plastic lid. Thread a string through the hole and tie the ends together in a single overhand knot. Mix white glue and enough food coloring to produce a deep blue color. Spread about ½ tablespoon of the blue glue completely covering the plastic area inside the raised rim. Sprinkle sand into the wet glue across the bottom edge of the circle *(directly opposite the thread loop).* Cut seaweed from green paper and place on the wet glue.

To make the fish, cut paper into ¾" x 6" strips. Cut slits as indicated in illustration. Curve the strip around, sliding the two slits together to produce the body and tail of the fish. Arrange fish on the wet glue and let "aquarium" dry.

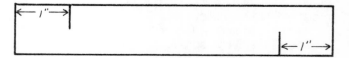

Paper Plate Lion

Ages: 4-7
Materials:
   9″ paper plate
   Construction paper: black for eyes and nose; orange, yellow, or brown for mane
   Crayons or spray paint
   Glue
   Stapler

Directions:
Color the top of the paper plate yellow. Use crayons or spray lightly with paint. Cut plate as indicated in illustration. Fold nose section along dotted line. Staple the top section at the rim of the plate to the lower section overlapping ½″. Cut eyes and nose from black paper and glue into place. If desired, add crayon details such as whiskers and mouth. Cut paper into ½″ x 3″ strips for the mane. Glue strips around the edge of the plate to complete the mane. As a variation, 3″ pieces of yarn could be used for the mane by older children instead of the paper strips.

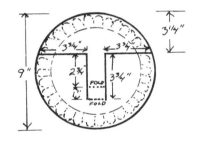

Paper Lion

Ages: 4-8
Materials:
   Construction paper: yellow and orange or brown and yellow
   Crayons
   Glue
   Stapler

Directions:
For the mane, fold a 9″ x 12″ piece of paper in half forming two 4½″ x 12″ sections. Fold the open 12″ sides one inch from the edge. Cut away a 1″ x 3½″ section from one end. *(See illustration.)* Fringe paper by beginning to cut through the folded edge and continuing to the top fold. Reverse one of the top folds. Overlap the two 1″ x 12″ sections and glue. Now glue the fringed section into a circle by slipping the tab at one end into the opposite fringed end and stapling to secure. To make the face, fold down the two top corners of a 4½″ x 4½″ piece of paper of a contrasting color. Use crayons to draw face. Glue face on top of mane.

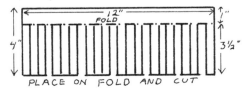

PLACE ON FOLD AND CUT

Underwater Scene

Ages: 6-10
Materials:
   Drawing paper with a smooth surface
   Crayons
   Blue water-based marker
   Sponge

Directions:
Draw an underwater scene using crayons. Include fish, seaweed, sandy bottom, shellfish, and shells. With the blue marker draw waves in the open spaces of the picture. Moisten a sponge with water squeezing out excess. Rub the sponge over the picture, once and in one direction, causing the blue marker to streak across the picture.

Stand-up Lion

Ages: 4-7
Materials:
   Construction paper: orange and yellow or brown and yellow
   Glue
   Crayons

Directions:
Fold a 9″ x 12″ piece of paper in half diagonally. Cut as indicated in illustration. Cut a 5″ circle from the contrasting color for the mane. Fringe mane. Cut a head using the same color as the body. Draw facial features. Glue head in center of mane. Glue or staple mane in place.

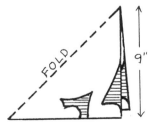

FOLD   9″

27

Tube Snake

Ages: 4-7
Materials:
    Cardboard tube from the center of a waxed paper or
        paper towel roll
    Markers
    Construction paper: red and black
    Glue

Directions:
  Use markers to decorate the tube. Cut along the seam line of the tube starting at one end and cutting to within one inch of the opposite end of the tube. Cut eyes and a "Y"-shaped tongue from paper. Glue eyes and tongue into place to complete.

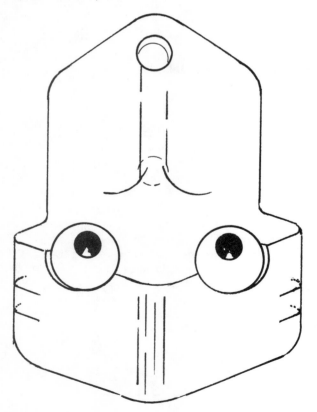

Spiral Snake

Ages: 4-9
Materials:
    Construction paper
    Markers or crayons

Directions:
  Round off the corners of a 9" x 12" piece of paper producing an oval shape. Starting in the center of one of the sides cut the oval in a spiral fashion making the snake's body 1½" wide. The small oval in the center will become the snake's head. A notch in the head can be cut for the mouth. *(Pre-cut snakes for preschoolers and draw pencil lines following the preceding instructions for children ages 6 and 7.)*
  After the snake is cut, details can be added to both sides of the snake with crayons or markers. If desired, eyes and tongue can be cut from paper of contrasting colors and glued into place.

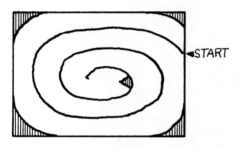

Milk Jug Frog

Ages: 4-7
Materials:
    Plastic gallon milk jug with circular or oval indentations
    Green spray paint
    Green polyester fabric or felt
    Construction paper: black and white
    Plastic model glue
    Stapler

Directions:
  Prepare the jug by cutting as indicated in illustration, including the side slits. Spray the inside of the jug with a very light coat of paint. Cut the two leg pieces from the fabric using pattern 58C. Thread fabric legs through the side slots. Position each fabric piece so that two legs of equal length are produced on the outside of the frog. Cut two white circles and two slightly smaller black circles. Glue black circles in center of white circles for eyes. Then glue these over the indentations and staple through the plastic to help secure.
  These frogs make good storage containers for crayons or small toys.

Self Portrait

Ages: 4-7
Materials:
  Drawing paper
  Crayons

Directions:
  Draw the outline of a head, neck and shoulders on a 9″ x 12″ piece of drawing paper. Have the child complete the outline using crayons to draw a face which represents himself. Before the children begin to work, see how many parts of their faces they can name. This should add to the detail and interest of their individual self portraits.
Variation:
  Add an adhesive bandage someplace on the drawing. Talk about the wonderful bodies God has given us which can heal cuts and bruises.

Day and Night Pictures

Ages: 5-7
Materials:
  Drawing paper
  Crayons

Directions:
  Fold a 9″ x 12″ piece of paper in half dividing it into two 9″ x 6″ sections. With the fold on the left, cut away a 2½″ x 6″ section from the top of the front panel. Use crayon to color the remaining front section as a blanket or glue a 6½″ x 6″ piece of colored construction paper or fabric over the drawing paper. Unfold the paper and trace pattern 62A of the child on the 9″ x 6″ back panel so that the child's chin will rest on the top of the blanket. Use crayons to color the child doing something he would enjoy while he is awake and playing. Talk about how God watches over us while we sleep and play.

Doorknob Nose Face

Ages: 4-6
Materials:
  9″ paper plate
  Assorted construction paper or crayons
  Yarn
  Single-edged razor blade

Directions:
  Cut slashes in the center of a paper plate with the razor blade. *(See illustration.)* Test to see if the plate will slip over a doorknob. Make the slashes longer if necessary, but the plate should fit snuggly on the doorknob. With crayons draw eyes above and a smile below the slashes. If desired, eyes and mouth can also be cut from construction paper. For hair, glue 2″ pieces of yarn around the edge of the top half of the plate. The face can be placed over a doorknob with the doorknob becoming the nose of the face.

Footprints

Ages: 5-8
Materials:
  Powdered tempera
  Powdered laundry detergent
  Flat dish
  Construction paper

Directions:
  Mix one part powdered tempera, one part powdered laundry detergent, and one part water. Place a small amount of this paint in a flat dish. Make a fist and then dip the little finger side of the fist into the paint. Print a "foot" onto the paper. Continue to dip into the paint and print feet. Print five toes for each foot by dipping an index finger into the paint and using it to print five toes.

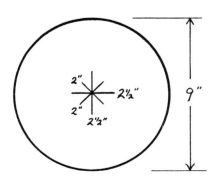

PAPER BAG HOUSE

Ages: 5-7
Materials:
   Paper lunch bag
   Crayons
   1" x 3" piece of construction paper (chimney)
   Half-sheet of newspaper
   Stapler

Directions:
   Fold down the top 3" of a paper bag. Color this folded down section as a roof. Draw windows and doors on the lower portion of the bag. Crumple newspaper and place it inside the bag. Fold down roof and staple bag shut. Glue or staple chimney into place.

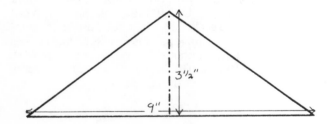

HOUSE

Ages: 5-8
Materials:
   Drawing paper
   Construction paper: red and brown
   Glue
   Crayons

Directions:
   Cut an 8" x 12" piece of drawing paper and fold it in half to produce two 8" x 6" sections. Make a chimney from a 1" x 2" strip of red paper. Cut a roof from a piece of brown paper as shown in the illustration.
   Glue the roof onto the drawing paper along the folded edge. Glue chimney in place. With crayons, decorate the house's exterior. Open the drawing paper and draw a family inside.

STAND-UP HOUSE

Ages: 5-7
Materials:
   Drawing paper
   Construction paper
   Crayons
   Glue

Directions:
   Draw a picture of a family or something to express love, kindness, or obedience in the center of a 9" x 12" piece of paper using the 12" sides as the top and bottom of the picture. Fold the picture in half producing two 6" x 9" sections. Fold back 1" tabs on the open 9" sides. Cut another 9" x 12" piece of drawing paper as indicated in diagram. Glue a 3" x 6" piece of construction paper over door. Add a circular construction paper doorknob. Glue 3" x 9" piece of construction paper onto roof section. Trim to make the paper fit the shape of the roof.
   Glue on a 1½" x 4" strip for a chimney. Glue tabs of 9" x 12" paper onto back of house. Open door to look inside.

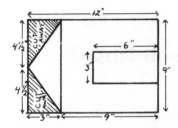

SIMPLE HOUSE

Ages: 4-7
Materials:
   Construction paper: black and red
   Drawing paper
   Glue Crayons

Directions:
   Cut a house shape as indicated in the illustration from a 9" x 12" piece of drawing paper. Cut two 1" x 7½" strips of black paper and one 1½" x 4" piece of red paper. Glue the black strips on to represent the roof and the red strip to represent a chimney. Draw a family portrait or the exterior of a house.

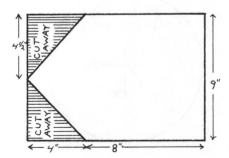

Peephole Picture

Ages: 5-8
Materials:
 Drawing paper and/or construction paper
 Glue
 Crayons

Directions:
 Fold in half a 9" x 10" piece of paper producing two 9" x 5" sections. Fold back 1" flaps on both 9" ends. This will be the front sheet, so cut an opening from the center fold. Suggested shapes are a heart, circle, or rectangle.
 Fold a 9" x 12" piece of drawing paper in half producing two 9" x 6" sections. Unfold and draw a picture on the paper using the 12" sides as the top and bottom of the picture. Place the smaller paper in front of the picture and glue the flaps of the smaller paper to the back of the picture.
Suggestions for use:
1. Above a heart opening on the front sheet print "God loves" and have the children draw self portraits on the back sheet.
2. Above the heart opening on the front sheet print "Happy Mother's Day" or Happy Father's Day" and have the children draw self portraits of themselves and their parents.
3. Make the circular opening become the "O" in "You". Print "Thank" above the opening, "You" with the circular opening being the "O", and "God" below the opening. On the back sheet have the children draw something for which they are thankful.

Suncatcher

Ages: 8-10
Materials:
 White glue
 Rug yarn
 Plastic lid from a half-pound margarine tub
 Assorted seeds, spices, and dried flowers

Directions:
 Glue a piece of rug yarn around the inside rim of the plastic lid. Loop one end of the yarn in a circle for a hanger. Let the glue dry. Place approximately one tablespoon of glue inside the yarn and spread evenly. Add more glue if necessary. Arrange the dried materials onto the glue. Allow to dry at least two days. When the glue is completely dry, peel the suncatcher from the plastic lid and hang in a window.

Good Deed Beads

Ages: Suggestion 1: 6-7
 Suggestion 2: 8-10
Materials:

Suggestion 1	*Suggestion 2*
Construction paper	Wallpaper
30" piece of yarn	30" piece of thread
Cellophane tape	Glue
Tapestry needle	Toothpick or nail
	Tapestry needle

Directions:
Suggestion 1
 Cut various colors of construction paper into 4½" x 1½" strips. Have the children print on separate strips between six and ten good deeds which they can do at home. Wrap strip around a pencil, tape the end, and carefully slide the bead off the pencil. Continue forming beads from the rest of the strips. Thread yarn into the needle and string the beads onto the yarn. Tie the ends of the yarn together to complete the necklace.
Suggestion 2
 Cut wallpaper in varying sizes of rectangular and triangular shapes. Roll the wallpaper around the nail or toothpick so that the bright color is on the outside. The point of the triangle should be on the outside. Glue the ends and slide the bead off the nail or toothpick. Using a needle and thread, string the completed beads together. If desired, good deeds can be written on the inside of the wallpaper strips before they are rolled into beads.

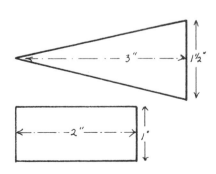

Pencil Holder

Ages: 7-9
Materials:

Suggestion 1
  Soup can
  Masking tape
  Brown shoe polish
  Paper towels

Suggestion 2
  Soup can
  White glue
  Small pieces of calico
  Rickrack

Directions:

Suggestion 1

Tear masking tape into pieces ½" to ¾" long. Cover the entire outside of the can with pieces of tape overlapping edges to insure complete coverage. Rub a light coat of brown shoe polish over the masking tape and buff off any excess polish with a paper towel.

Suggestion 2

Dilute the glue by mixing one part glue with one part water. Paint a small area of the can with the diluted glue and lay pieces of fabric over the painted areas. Continue until the entire can is covered with fabric overlapping edges to insure complete coverage. To complete, paint a top coat of diluted glue over the fabric and glue a piece of rickrack around the top and bottom of the can.

Gifts

Ages: 4-8
Materials:
  Drawing paper
  Construction paper

Directions:

Fold a 9" x 12" piece of paper in half producing two 6" x 9" sections. Glue on a ½" x 9" and a ½" x 6" strip of construction paper to represent the ribbon on a gift package. To form a bow, glue a ½" x 9" strip into a circle. Glue the circle onto the center of the package. Press and glue the top and bottom of the circle together forming the two loops of the bow. Also glue two ½" x 2" strips from the center of the bow for the ribbon's ends.

Suggestions for use:

1. Have children draw a picture of one of the gifts God has given them on the inside of the "gift."
2. Have children print a Scripture verse and draw a picture on the inside of the "gift." Give to a shut-in.
3. Place a photograph of the child on the inside of the "gift." Give to parents as a Christmas gift.

Bookmarks

Ages: 7-10
Materials:
  Construction paper
  Clear Contact paper
  Suggestion 1: dried pressed flowers and glue
  Suggestion 2: bleach and leaves, newsprint

Directions:

Suggestion 1

Arrange the flowers on the construction paper and glue in place with a small amount of glue. Add a Bible verse or a personal message if desired. Peel backing from the Contact paper and lay the sticky side on top of bookmark flowers. Trim away excess edges of the Contact paper.

Suggestion 2

Choose a dark or bright shade of construction paper. Brush bleach over the vein side of a leaf. Place leaf on a clean sheet of newsprint and lay construction paper over the bleached side of the leaf. Rub the construction paper gently and then carefully remove. Add a Bible verse or personal message if desired. Peel backing from the Contact paper and lay the sticky side on top of the bookmark. Trim away excess edges.

Note Holder

Ages: 4-10

Materials:

    Wooden spring clothespin
    Green spray paint
    Silk flower approximately 1½"–2" in diameter
    Silk leaves approximately 1½" long
    1" piece of adhesive-backed magnetic tape
    Tacky craft glue

Directions:

Spray paint clothespin and let dry. Peel the paper from the magnetic tape. Place the tape onto the upper portion, above the metal spring, of the clothespin. On the other side of the clothespin, glue two leaves onto the bottom section. If the flower has a raised plastic back, cut the plastic off as close to the flower as possible. The flower may tend to fall apart without this back, so glue it to the top portion of the clothespin. As the glue dries, have the children write a special note to their mothers to clip in the note holder.

Wooden Bead Vase

Ages: 7-10

Materials:

    Wooden bead approximately 1½" in height
    Modeling clay
    Small flowers *(Silk, dried, or plastic flowers with stiff stems, baby's breath, statice, etc.)*

Directions:

Fill the hole of the bead two-thirds with clay. Arrange flowers in bead by pushing the stems into the clay. Small holes for the stems may be made in the clay with toothpicks. Use to decorate a table or chest.

YARN HEART

Ages: 6-10
Materials:
  Red rug yarn
  White glue
  Waxed paper
  Drawing paper

Directions:
Draw the outline of a heart onto the drawing paper. Place a piece of waxed paper over the drawing paper. Lay the yarn along the outline and cut the yarn to the exact length required to cover the heart outline. Mix one part glue and one part water. Dip the yarn into the mixture. Squeeze excess glue from yarn. Lay the yarn on top of the waxed paper along the outline. Put several drops of full strength glue over the yarn where the two ends meet. Let dry on the waxed paper for at least one day.

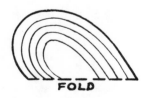
FOLD

CONCENTRIC HEARTS

Ages: 8-10
Materials:
  Construction paper: red and white
  Glue

Directions:
Fold a 9″ x 6″ piece of red paper in half forming two 4½″ x 6″ sections. Cut a heart from the folded paper. Keeping the paper folded, cut at least four concentric hearts. *(See illustration.)* Discard the center solid heart. Open hearts, arrange, and glue hearts onto the white paper.

HEART BASKET

Ages: 6-8
Materials:
  Red construction paper
  Stapler
  Optional: white tempera and heart-shaped sponge stamp

Directions:
From the red paper cut two 2½″ x 9″ strips and one 1″ x 9″ strip. Fold each 2½″ x 9″ strip in half producing two 2½″ x 4½″ sections. Round off both corners of the open ends of each strip. Fit the two folded sections together *(slide C between A and B)* to produce a pocket and a heart shape. *(See illustration.)* Glue overlapping sections. Next glue the 1″ x 9″ strip to the top *(open)* end of the heart to produce a handle. If desired a white "lace" heart can be easily stamped onto the basket with white tempera paint and a heart-shaped sponge stamp.

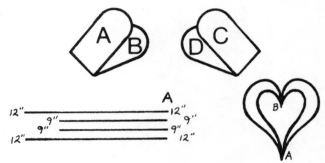

PAPER HEART

Ages: 6-10
Materials:
  Red construction paper
  White tissue paper
  Glue
  Stapler

Directions:
Cut two 1″ x 9″ strips and two 1″ x 12″ strips from red paper. Lay the two 1″ x 9″ strips directly on top of each other. Place one 1″ x 12″ strip above and one strip below the 1″ x 9″. *(See illustration.)* Even up all four ends at one end and staple the strips together. Bend the two open ends of the 12″ strips around to form a heart. As you hold the 12″ strips in place, bend the two open ends of the 9″ strips to form a second heart inside the first heart. Even up the ends of these four strips. Staple at B.

Cut the white tissue into 1″ squares. Place the eraser end of a pencil on the center of a tissue square. Crush the tissue around the pencil. While still on the pencil, dip the tissue into glue and then position on the outside of the heart.

Stars and Stripes

Ages: 6-10
Materials:
    White construction paper
    Tagboard
    Blue crayon
    Red tempera
    Small sponge clipped in a spring-type clothespin

Directions:

Cut out stars from the tagboard using pattern 56B. With a pencil trace a pleasing arrangement of stars onto the white paper. Go over the traced lines with heavy blue crayoned lines. Dilute the red tempera by adding water so that it does not cover, but rather beads off the crayoned lines. Dip the sponge into the tempera and make parallel stripes across the paper.

Paper Star

Ages: 6-8
Materials:
    Yellow construction paper
    Glue
    Stapler

Directions:

Fold a 9" x 12" piece of yellow paper in half producing two 4½" x 12" sections. Lay pattern 56A on the folded paper so that the star's points lie along the folded edge. Trace and cut along the lines. Fold the solid open edges toward the center along the dotted lines on the pattern. Overlap and glue the folded edge sections. Bring the two ends together overlapping the tab to form a circle. Staple to hold in place.

Wreath Plate

Ages: 3-6
Materials:
    9" Styrofoam plate
    Green crayon
    Red construction paper
    Glue

Directions:

Trace and then cut a 3½" diameter circle from the center of the plate. Color both sides of the plate with green crayon. Cut the inside and outside edges as shown in the illustration. Bake on a cookie sheet at 400° until the plate just begins to curl. Remove quickly and cool. Glue on holly berries and bow cut from red paper.

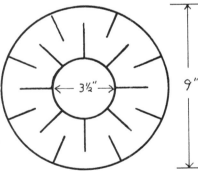

Glitter String Designs

Ages: 6-10
Materials:
    Blue construction paper
    Red glitter
    Silver gummed stars
    Glue
    Telephone book or large catalog
    String

Directions:

Fold the blue paper in half and then unfold. Dip all but the 6" end of a 30" piece of string into glue. *(If you are making more than one picture, reuse the same string.)* Squeeze the excess glue from the string. Lay the string on the blue paper in a random pattern on one side of the middle fold. Fold the paper shut over the string. Lay a telephone book or catalog on top of the paper. Pull out the string. Open the paper and quickly sprinkle paper with red glitter. Shake off excess glitter. Arrange gummed stars around glitter design.

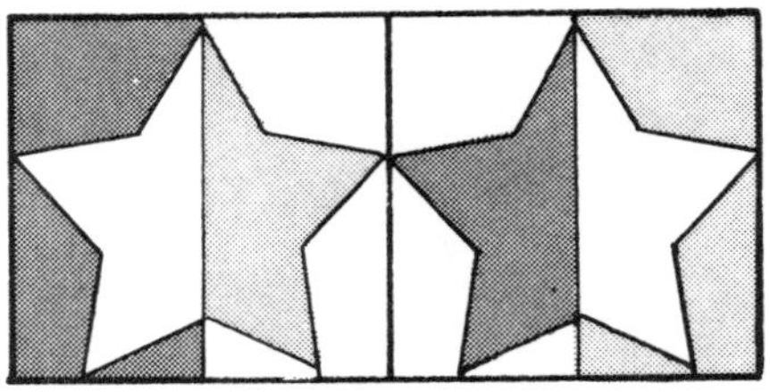

Patriotic Stars

Ages: 6-10
Materials:
    Construction paper: red, white, and blue
    Glue

Directions:

Cut one 6" x 12" piece of white paper, one 6" x 3" piece of red paper, and 6" x 3" piece of blue paper. Trace the half-star pattern 56C on the red and blue pieces. Cut out the stars. Arrange them on the white paper as indicated in the diagram. After all the pieces are properly arranged, glue them into place.

Candy Cane

Ages: 5-7
Materials:
Newsprint
Red crayon
Glue
Red and green construction paper

Directions:
Cut the newsprint into a square. With a red crayon color a ⅓" - ½" border along two sides. *(See illustration.)* Turn the paper crayoned side down. Starting at corner A begin rolling paper toward corner B. Roll entire paper into a tight tube. Glue outside corner to the tube. Bend the tube into a candy cane shape. If desired, make holly leaves and berries for trim from the red and green paper. Glue trim onto candy cane.

Glitter Star

Ages: 4-8
Materials:
Clear plastic lid (no lettering) from margarine tub or frozen topping container
Christmas sticker
Glue
Darning needle
Thread
Transparent glitter

Directions:
Using pattern 58B, cut a star shape from the plastic lid. With a darning needle, poke a hole through the plastic near the top point. Draw the thread through the hole and tie the ends together. Spread a thin layer of glue over the entire top surface of the star. Place a sticker on the glue in the center of the star. Sprinkle the star with glitter and then shake off the excess.

Circular Paper Star

Ages: 6-10
Materials:
Yellow construction paper
Glue
Christmas stickers
Paper punch
Thread

Directions:
Cut a circle using pattern 59A. Cut the circle as indicated, dividing the circle in five equal sections. Place a thin line of glue along the outside rim of one section. Fold the outside rim in half, press the two glued halves together, and hold until the glue sets. Repeat this procedure on the remaining four sections. To shape stars, flatten each point by pressing down on the glued portion. The sections should be creased, not depressed. If desired, a Christmas sticker may be placed in the center of the star. Also, a hole may be punched through the top point and a thread hanger can be used.

Candle

Ages: 8-10
Materials:
Glass or small jar
Votive candle
Tissue paper—pastel shades
White glue
Brush

Directions:
Cut several shades of pastel tissue paper into small square pieces. Pieces should measure about 1". Also cut a cross from a contrasting dark or bright piece of tissue paper. Paint a small area of the jar with diluted glue (one part glue and two parts water). Quickly cover the painted area with small pieces of pastel tissue. Continue painting and covering small areas until the entire jar is covered with tissue. Paint a thin coat of diluted glue over the entire jar. Place the cross on the wet jar. Do not paint the cross with glue as the dark shades of tissue sometimes fade and run.
Variation:
For Christmas cut a Christmas motif (star, tree) from the dark tissue and follow the preceding directions.

CHRISTMAS TREE

Ages: 6-9
Materials:
- Green construction paper
- Glue
- Christmas sticker
- Optional: crayon shavings, iron, and newsprint

Directions:

Fold a 9″ x 12″ piece of green paper in half producing two 4½″ x 12″ sections. Using pattern 60B, trace and cut out tree. If desired, trim the tree with crayon shavings which will be its ornaments. First sprinkle crayon shavings on one side of the tree. Fold shut, cover with a sheet of newsprint, and press with a warm iron.

Reverse the fold on the tree only. Bend the base around behind the tree and staple ends together. Place a sticker in the center of the base directly behind the opening.

STRING CROSS

Ages: 8-10
Materials:
- 9″ x 12″ tagboard or poster board
- Darning or tapestry needle
- Crochet thread
- Cellophane tape

Directions:

Draw a cross, as indicted in the illustration, on the poster board. Mark off all lines into ¼″ sections. Use a needle to punch a hole at each ¼″ mark. *(Note: if you are making more than one, use this copy as a pattern.)* Attach the pattern piece to a second 9″ x 12″ piece of poster board with paper clips and use a needle to poke holes through the pattern sheet and into the second sheet.

Making the design:

Top sections: tape the end of a 30″ piece of thread near the #1 hole of the vertical line. Push threaded needle through #1 on the horizontal line and bring it back through #1 of the vertical line. Thread it through #2 of the vertical line and bring it back through #2 on the horizontal line. Continue in a similar manner until both #8 holes are connected with thread. On the front side (the side without pattern lines or numbers) connect hole #8 to hole #0 with one long stitch on the vertical line and connect hole #0 with hole #1 on the horizontal line with one long stitch. Complete the other top section in the same manner. *(Note: if you run out of thread, tape the end to the back and tape a new piece to the back as you continue sewing.)*

Bottom sections: Connect the two A's, the two B's, the two C's, etc. as explained above. Complete by connecting point X and point A of the horizontal line, and point X and point L on the vertical line. Complete the other bottom section in the same manner.

CROSS EGG

Ages: 4-8
Materials:
- Hard-boiled egg
- Cellophane tape
- Food coloring
- Vinegar
- Paper towels

Directions:

Place two strips of tape on the egg to produce a cross shape. Make sure that the tape is pressed tightly against the egg. Mix one cup water, one tablespoon vinegar, and sufficient food coloring to produce desired color. Place the egg in the food coloring dye. When desired shade is reached, remove egg and dry it with a paper towel. Carefully remove the tape to reveal a white cross.

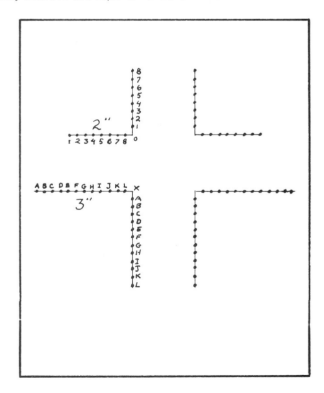

Ribbon Bookmark

Ages: 4-7
Materials:
Satin-backed velvet or suede ribbon 1⅜" wide
Lace ribbon ⅝" wide
Glue

Directions:
Cut a 4½" piece of velvet ribbon. Cut one end in an inverted "V" shape. Cut a 1¼" and 3½" piece of the lace ribbon. Glue the two pieces of lace ribbon onto the velvet ribbon in a cross shape.

Paper Cross

Ages: 5-10
Materials:
Construction paper
Stapler
Glue

Directions:
Cut two 1" x 12" strips and two 1" x 8" strips from paper. Fold the two shorter strips in half. Unfold. Lay the two 1" x 12" strips directly on top of each other. Place one 1" x 8" strip above and one 1" x 8" strip below the two larger strips. Even up the ends on one end. Staple all strips together at the midpoint of the shorter strips (at the fold). Fold a ¾" tab at the end of each strip. Overlap and glue tabs on each 8" strip to form side bars of the cross. Pinch sides of strips together near stapled end to help shape. Overlap and glue tabs to form top and bottom sections of the cross.

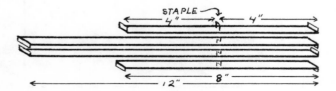

Pilgrim Girl Hat

Ages: 4-6
Materials:
12" x 18" piece of white construction paper
Stapler

Directions:
Cut paper as indicated in illustration. Bring corner A around and staple it on top of corner B. Bring corner C around and staple it on top of corner D.

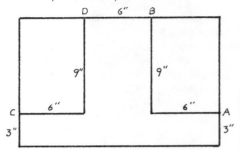

Pilgrim Boy Hat

Ages: 4-6
Materials:
Construction paper: black and yellow
Glue

Directions:
Round the corners of a 12" square piece of black paper making a circle. Cut and fold the center section of the circle as indicated in the illustration. Fold a 3" square of yellow paper in half. Cut the center as shown in the illustration to make a buckle. Center and glue buckle along the fold of the center section.
Note: If the hat is too small for some children, cut several slits into the inside edges of hat.

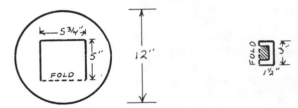

Holey Bookmark

Ages: 8-10
Materials:
Construction paper: two contrasting colors
Paper punch
Glue

Directions:
From one color of paper cut a 2" x 5" strip and from the other color cut a 1½" x 4½" strip. With a pencil draw a cross onto the smaller piece. Punch holes evenly spaced along the lines of the cross. Center the smaller piece on the larger piece, pencil lines down, and glue.

Cornucopia

Ages: 6-8
Materials:

9″ x 12″ piece of construction paper: brown or yellow
Stapler
Assorted construction paper or pictures of fruits and vegetables

Directions:

Fold paper in half producing two 6″ x 9″ sections. Fringe as indicated in the diagram. Make fringe sections about ¾″ wide. Open the paper, and staple corner 1 on top of corner 2. Also staple the center of side B over the center of side C.

Provide construction paper from which fruit and vegetable shapes can be cut or provide pictures of fruits and vegetables. Glue the pictures of food in the cornucopia.

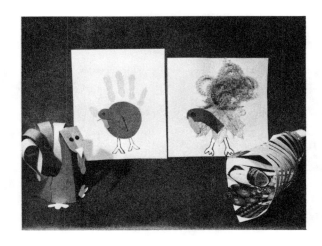

Tube Turkey

Ages: 7-10
Materials:

Construction paper
Glue

Directions:

Using pattern 58A, cut the turkey's head and body from a folded 9″ x 12″ piece of brown paper. Overlap and glue ends together to form tube-shaped body. Bend down the top of the head along dotted lines on pattern. Cut five 1″ x 9″ strips from various fall colors for feathers. Bend these strips into loops and glue around the back portion of the body. Also cut eyes, wattle, beak, wings, and feet from paper. Glue these body parts in place.

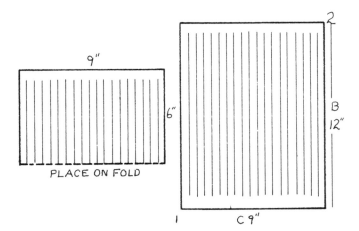

Turkey

Ages: 6-10
Materials:

Construction paper
Glue
Assorted dried materials (body: maple leaf; feathers: ornamental grasses, wheat, oats, or various dried weeds found on a nature walk)

Directions:

Arrange and glue the dried materials for feathers in center top of a 9″ x 12″ piece of paper. Glue a leaf, which has been dried for several days between the pages of an old book, over the feathers. Cut a head, beak, wattle, eyes, and feet from paper and glue the pieces into place.

Hand-print Turkey

Ages: 3-6
Materials:

Construction paper
Tempera
Glue

Directions:

Place a small amount of paint onto a plate which is larger than the hands of the children. Dip hand into paint and lay hand flat pressing it onto a piece of paper. As the paint dries, cut a body, head, feet, eyes, beak, and wattle from paper and then glue into place.

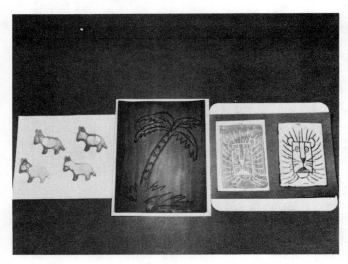

CRAYON RESISTS

Ages: 5-10
Materials:
   Drawing or construction paper
   Tempera
   Sponge or large brush
   Newsprint
   Crayons

Directions:
   Draw a picture with crayons pressing hard enough to produce waxy lines. Use a large brush or a small sponge to apply paint. The picture must be quickly painted over only once. Do not continue to paint and repaint the same area. Also, the tempera paint must be diluted with water. Test tempera over a practice sheet on which crayon lines have been drawn to see if it has been thinned enough with water. If the tempera is too concentrated, it will cover the picture.
Picture Suggestions:
1. Use black crayon on black paper and give a yellow wash of tempera.
2. For snow scenes use blue crayon on blue paper and give a white wash of tempera.
3. A black tempera wash over a picture on drawing paper could depict numerous Biblical stories which took place at night.
4. Use a blue tempera wash over an underwater picture for Jonah.
5. Use a brown tempera wash over a picture of Jeremiah at the base of a long narrow piece of paper. The drawing paper would represent the cistern and the paint would represent the mud.
6. Make a picture of Saul on drawing paper. Use yellow tempera over and around the area where Saul is in the picture to represent the light from Heaven.

STYROFOAM PRINTS

Ages: 7-10
Materials:
   Styrofoam food trays or disposable plates
   Tempera
   Large brush or brayer
   Drawing paper

Directions:
   Cut away the raised rim of the plate or tray. Cut the styrofoam into a rectangular shape. With a dull pencil, draw a picture on the foam. Press firmly so that indentations are made by the pencil lines. (Note: any words used must be printed backwards.) Use a brayer or large brush to cover the Styrofoam drawing with thick tempera to which a small amount of liquid dishwashing detergent has been added. Lay a slightly larger piece of paper over the styrofoam and rub the top of the paper gently. Carefully remove the print.
Suggestions for use:
1. Draw an animal. Print and mount together two copies to represent the pair of animals which Noah took with him on the ark.
2. Fold paper. Make prints on front of folded sheet to make greeting cards or stationery.

COOKIE CUTTER PRINTS

Ages: 4-7
Materials:
   Cookie cutters
   Tempera
   Construction paper
   Drawing paper

Directions:
   1. Use tempera with a thick consistency. Place ¼" of tempera into a shallow container with a flat bottom which is big enough to accommodate the cookie cutters. Dip the cutter into the paint and then use it to print several shapes. Press firmly over entire cookie cutter as you print.
   2. Use tempera with a thick consistency. Add enough liquid dishwashing detergent to make a bubble film across the cookie cutter when it is dipped into the paint. Use cookie cutters with open tops (sides only) for this type of printing. Place ⅛" to ¼" of paint in a shallow container. Dip cutter into paint being sure there is a film of soap and paint across the inside of the cutter. Press the cutter onto the paper. If the soap film does not break, touch it with your finger before lifting cookie cutter.

Vegetable Prints

Ages: 4-10
Materials:
    Vegetables
    Tempera
    Brush
    Drawing paper or construction paper

Directions:

Mix a few drops of liquid dishwashing detergent into the tempera. Prepare the vegetable to be used as a stamp. As you cut through the vegetable, make sure the printing surface is even so the entire printing surface touches the paper when printing. Dip the vegetable into a shallow amount of paint. Press firmly onto the paper.

Vegetable suggestions:
1. Use a celery stem to print the scales on a fish shape.
2. Use a potato and carve any desired shape into the printing surface.
3. Use an onion to print a flower.
4. Use broccoli or cauliflower to print a tree.

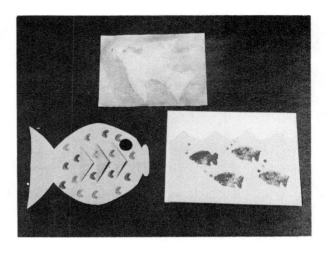

Sponge Stamps

Ages: 4-7
Materials:
    Sponge
    Wooden spools or small wooden blocks
    Glue *(not water soluble)*
    Tempera
    Drawing or construction paper

Directions:

Construct sponge stamps prior to class. Trace any pattern 62B onto the sponge. Moisten the sponge with water to soften and then cut out the shape with scissors. Let the sponge dry. Then glue it onto the spool or block.

Mix a small amount of tempera, water, and a few drops of liquid detergent. Place a small amount of paint (no deeper than ½") in a shallow container. Dip the stamp into the paint and use it to print several shapes before dipping into the paint again. Wash sponge and store for reuse.

Sponge suggestions:
1. Cut sponge into a fish shape. Print on blue paper scalloped across the top to represent waves. Bubbles can be printed by dipping the end of a drinking straw into blue paint.
2. Cut sponge into a free-form shape. Print to make altar or well.
3. Cut sponge into a heart shape and with white tempera print lacey white hearts on red paper.
4. Cut bells, trees, or stars and print on newsprint to make Christmas wrapping paper.

Shortening Resists

Ages: 7-10
Materials:
    Newsprint or typing paper
    Solid vegetable shortening
    Cotton-tipped swabs
    Food coloring
    Large brush or sponge
    Newsprint
    Waxed paper

Directions:

Place ½ teaspoon of shortening on a small piece of waxed paper. Dip one end of cotton swab into the shortening. Use swab to draw picture on paper. Apply enough shortening to make the paper transparent where the picture has been drawn. When the picture is complete, use the clean end of the swab to wipe away any excess shortening. Place picture on newspaper and print entire surface with food coloring which has been diluted with water. Mount pictures on windows where light can shine through the transparent areas.

Picture suggestions:
1. Draw Moses' shining face after he talked with God at the burning bush.
2. Draw a snow scene with crayons and fill in the areas covered with snow with the shortening. Paint with blue food coloring.

Sponge Painting

Ages: 4-7
Materials:
Tempera
Construction or drawing paper
Small pieces of sponge
Spring-type clothespins

Directions:
Place a small amount of tempera (no deeper than ¼")
in a shallow container. Clip sponge into clothespin. Dip
sponge into paint and then onto the paper. Print with an
up-and-down movement. Do not rub the sponge back
and forth over the paper as you would with a brush.
Picture suggestions:
1. Use precut shapes such as leaves, butterflies, animals, and snowmen.
2. Draw a picture with crayons. Use the sponge printing for accent color such as autumn leaves and blossoms on a tree.

Comb Prints

Ages: 6-8
Materials:
Drawing paper
Crayons
Blue tempera
Comb

Directions:
Complete a picture on drawing paper with crayons.
Suggest that black storm clouds be included across the
top of the paper. Place no more than a ¼" of paint in a
container that is big enough in which to dip the comb. Dip
the teeth of the comb into the paint. Starting at the top of
the paper, rub the teeth of the comb down across the
paper. Dip the comb into the paint several times and
continue to paint "rain" always beginning from the top of
the paper.
Picture suggestions:
1. Draw the ark in the water or on dry land.
2. Draw a spring picture.

Blown Paint

Ages: 6-10
Materials:
Food coloring or tempera diluted with water
Paper with a smooth surface
Straw
Eyedropper or spoon
Newspaper

Directions:
Cover work area with newspaper. Using a teaspoon or
eyedropper put about ¼ teaspoon of paint near the bottom of the paper. Blow the paint across the paper by
blowing through a drinking straw held close to, but not
touching, the paint. Move the straw to follow the paint as it
moves across the paper. If desired, additional drops of
paint can be added and then blown across the paper.
Allow paint to dry.
Picture suggestions:
1. Use green paint for stems and leaves. Add flowers
   made from paper, tissue, paint prints, or drawn with
   crayon.
2. Use brown paint for a tree. Tear green paper into small
   pieces for leaves and then glue them on the tree. Put
   Zaccheus in the tree.

Foil Pictures

Ages: 7-10
Materials:
 Aluminum foil
 Tempera
 Liquid dishwashing detergent
 Small sponge or large brush
 Newspaper

Directions:

Cut foil into rectangular pieces no larger than 6″ x 9″. Dilute the tempera with water producing a thin consistency. Add one teaspoon of liquid dishwashing detergent for each ¼ cup of paint. Paint the foil and allow to dry.

Place foil on a section of newspaper. Draw a picture on the foil with a dull pencil. The foil will tear if the pencil is pressed too hard or if the pencil is too sharp. Glue foil onto a slightly larger piece of construction paper.

Marble Prints

Ages: 4-10
Materials:
 Construction or drawing paper
 Tempera—two contrasting colors
 Marbles
 Cardboard box
 Spoon

Directions:

Place tempera into small dishes. In each dish put two or three marbles. Roll the marbles in the paint until they are completely covered with paint. Put a piece of paper in the bottom of a cardboard box. The box bottom should be only slightly larger than the paper. With a spoon, lift the marbles from the paint and place in the box. Tilt the sides of the box and let the marbles roll over the box bottom forming a random pattern on the paper.

Picture suggestions:

1. Cut a silhouette of a stained glass window from black paper. Glue over printed paper and trim to fit.
2. Place ½ teaspoon of yellow paint in the center of a piece of construction paper. With the spoon spread the paint in a circle with a diameter of about 2″. Place several clean marbles in the circle of paint and roll until the paint is streaked over the paper. Use blue paper to represent the sky and yellow paint to represent the sun. Cut flower shapes from pastel shades of paper and paint the center as above.

String Painting

Ages: 4-10
Materials:
 Construction or drawing paper
 Tempera
 30″ piece string or yarn
 Sponge
 Telephone book or large catalog

Directions:

Fold a piece of paper in half. Holding one end, dip the string into the tempera so that all but six inches in your hand is submerged in the paint. As you remove the string, squeeze the excess paint from the string with a small sponge. Open the folded paper and let the string fall in a random pattern on one side of the fold. Fold the paper shut. Place the book over the paper and slowly pull out the string.

Picture suggestions:

1. For a patriotic theme use blue paper and red paint. When the paint is dry, glue on silver star stickers.
2. For a butterfly, pull the string out through a small notch cut into the middle of the fold. To do this, thread the end of the string without paint through the notch before the paper is folded shut. The procedure can be repeated with another color of paint and a second string to produce a two-color butterfly. Cut a butterfly's body, head, and antennae from black paper and glue over the center fold concealing the hole.

Paint Blots

Ages: 4-7
Materials:
Tempera
Eyedropper or squeeze bottle
Drawing or construction paper

Directions:
Thin tempera slightly with water. Fold paper in half. Open paper. With eyedropper or squeeze bottle place dots of the tempera on one side of the center fold. Fold paper shut and rub over the paper from the fold to the outside edges. Open paper.
Picture suggestions:
1. Use symmetrical precut shapes such as butterflies or leaves for making blots.
2. Try to discover objects or shapes in the blots.

Marbleized Colors

Ages: 5-10
Materials:
Food coloring in squeeze bottles
Paper with a smooth surface
Sponge or large brush
Crayons

Directions:
Draw a picture on the paper with crayons. Brush or sponge water over the area where the food coloring will be placed. Avoid excess water, and leave at least a 1″ margin on all sides dry. Immediately squeeze several drops of food coloring near the bottom of the moistened paper. Lift the bottom edge of the paper and let the food coloring run toward the top. Lay paper flat to dry.
Suggestions for use:
1. Use red and yellow food coloring to represent fire. Use for stories such as the fiery furnace, the burning bush, or Elijah's altar on Mount Carmel.
2. Use blue and green for water.

Scraped Paint

Ages: 4-7
Materials:
Tempera
Drawing paper
Eyedropper or squeeze bottle
Corrugated cardboard
Newspaper

Directions:
Place drawing paper on a sheet of newspaper. With eyedropper or squeeze bottle place lines and dots of several colors of tempera on the drawing paper. Cut a strip of cardboard at least as wide as the paper. Scrape over the surface of the paper with the cardboard blending the wet tempera together.
Picture suggestions:
1. Use red and orange paint to represent fire.
2. Use green and blue paint to represent the waves of a stormy sea.

Stencils

Ages: 5-10
Materials:
Permanent marker
Stencil (tagboard or lightweight plastic)
Tempera
Stiff bristled brush
Fabric or paper

Directions:
Simple stencils can easily be made by first tracing a pattern on the tagboard or plastic. *(Plastic can be wiped clean and is more durable for repeated use.)* Cut out design using a pair of manicure scissors or a single-edged razor blade.
Hold stencil tightly over paper or fabric and apply paint. A small amount of thick paint should be applied to the tip of the brush only. Then tap the brush with an up-and-down movement over the opening of the stencil. (Do not paint with a back and forth movement of the brush.)
Picture suggestions:
1. Fringe the edges of a small piece of fabric. Make bookmarks or Christmas ornaments.
2. Use two colors of paint to stencil the shape of a fall leaf.
3. Cut a stencil of flames and place it over a drawing of a bush (Moses) or an altar (Elijah at Mount Carmel).

Color Separation

Ages: 4-10
Materials:
   Coffee filters
   Food coloring - red and blue diluted with water or red
      and green diluted with water
   Construction paper
   Newsprint

Directions:
   Butterfly: Cut butterfly wings from the filter. Place filter
on newsprint. Use an eyedropper to place small drops of
food coloring on the filter. Glue on a body, head, and
antennae cut from a single piece of black paper.
   Flower: Fold filter in half three times as you would fold
paper to make a snowflake. Cut only the open edge to
produce a petal shape. Brush a single line of food coloring down the center of each petal. Glue a yellow paper
circle in the center.
   Turkey: Follow directions for the flower. Cut a turkey's
body, head, and feet from construction paper. Glue in
place.

Sidewalks and Walls

Ages: 3-6
Materials:
   Paint brushes
   Water

Directions:
   Place a small amount of water into unbreakable containers. Allow children to paint designs onto the sidewalks
or the surfaces of the exterior walls around the building in
an area safe from traffic. *(No photo.)*

Ironed Designs

Ages: 4-8
Materials:
   Food colorings in small squeeze bottles
   Waxed paper
   Iron
   Construction paper

Directions:
   Fold a piece of waxed paper in half. Open waxed
paper and place several drops of food coloring (one or
more colors) on the waxed paper on one side of the
center fold. Do not place food coloring drops close to the
edges of the waxed paper. Fold the waxed paper shut.
Rub firmly over the waxed paper with a paper towel. If
more food coloring is needed lift the top layer of waxed
paper and add more drops in the desired areas. Fold
shut and rub again. When a pleasing pattern is obtained,
cover the waxed paper with a single sheet of newsprint
and press with a warm iron.
Suggestions for use:
1. Use blue and green food coloring. After ironing, scallop one side of the waxed paper to represent waves.
   Glue on fish cut from construction paper.
2. After ironing, glue waxed paper behind a church window silhouette cut from black paper. Trim to fit.
3. Use red and yellow to represent fire. Cut ironed
   waxed paper in a free form to represent the pillar of
   fire.

Painting Tips

1. Always have a supply of newspaper to cover tables.

2. A plastic shower curtain can be used to cover the floor of the work area.

3. Add a small amount of liquid dishwashing detergent to tempera paints. It will help the paint adhere to most any surface and make clean up easier. However, do not add to paint when making crayon resists.

4. Lids from jars (peanut butter, mayonnaise, etc.) make good paint dishes when sponge painting. They are not easily tipped over and spilled.

5. Use half-pound margarine tubs for paint. They are unbreakable and disposable.

6. A small sponge piece can be clipped to a spring-type clothespin and used for painting.

7. A small bowl of soapy water, a washcloth, and a towel at the paint area can simplify cleaning hands.

8. A man's tee shirt can be useful as a painting shirt as it has no buttons or long sleeves.

9. When mixing dry tempera, start with a very small amount of water, then thin to proper consistency.

10. Inform parents in advance when you will be painting. They can dress their children accordingly.

Craft Recipes

Bread Dough Clay

Ingredients:
¼ cup salt
¾ cup hot water
2 cups flour

Directions:
Mix salt and water. Add one cup flour. Stir until well blended. Add remaining cup of flour a little at a time. Knead on a flat surface for several minutes. Store at room temperature for six to twelve hours in a plastic bag or airtight container.

Small detail pieces may be used as this clay fuses together when baked. Bake molded objects at 250 degrees until golden brown. Higher oven temperatures cause the dough to puff up. Use tempera, acrylic paints, or water based markers to decorate.
Suggestions:
1. Shape and mold ornaments for Christmas. Place half of a paper clip into moist clay as a hanger before baking.
2. Make small objects for refrigerator magnets. When completed, add a piece of magnetic plastic tape to the back.

Cornstarch Clay

Ingredients:
1 cup cornstarch
1½ cups baking soda
1 cup cold water

Directions:
Mix cornstarch and baking soda. Add water and mix well. Cook over low heat, stirring constantly, until the mixture boils and thickens. Cool and then knead. Store at room temperature no longer than one day in an airtight container. If a tinted clay is desired, add food coloring to the water before mixing it into the dry ingredients.

Air dry clay. Objects must be molded from a single piece because details which are added tend to fall off as the clay dries. If desired, make a small hole in the top of each shape by pressing a drinking straw through the clay. When dry, thread a string or ribbon through the hole and tie ends.
Suggestions for use:
1. Roll out clay on waxed paper. Use cookie cutter for basic shape. Make impressions into the moist clay with nails, paper clips, spoons, etc.
2. Press dry alphabet macaroni into moist clay to spell key phrases of Scripture verses.

Detergent Paint

Ingredients:
Powdered laundry detergent
Water

Directions:
Mix detergent and enough water to form a thick paste. Use toothpick or craft stick to apply detergent as an accent to a picture. Do not mix the soap and water until you are ready to use it because the detergent paint will harden in 5 to 10 minutes.
Suggestions for use:
1. Let the detergent paint represent snow in a winter scene drawn on blue paper.
2. Precut the shape of a dove or a sheep from white paper. Apply the detergent paint as feathers or wool.

Soap Clay

Ingredients:
Small slivers of bar soap
Water

Directions:
Use a meat grinder to grind small pieces of bar soap into a powder. While mixing, add water slowly to powdered soap until a workable clay-like consistency is obtained. Working on waxed paper, mold clay into a simple shape or flatten clay to about ½″ thickness and then cut to desired shape with an open metal cookie cutter. Allow to dry on waxed paper for several days.

Epsom Salt Paint

Ingredients:
One part epsom salts
One part water
Food coloring

Directions:
Mix epsom salts, water, and food coloring in a pan. Heat until the epsom salts completely dissolves. Cool. Store at room temperature in a closed container.

Paint with the mixture using a brush. As the paint dries crystals will form on the paper.
Suggestions for use:
1. Paint outlined shapes of autumn leaves. Then spread a small amount of a contrasting color of food coloring into the center of the leaf. Blow or brush lightly to help spread the color.
2. Omit the food coloring and paint over a winter picture drawn in crayon. Transparent crystals will form as the epsom salt paint dries.

Salt Paint
Ingredients:
Two parts salt
One part flour
Water
Food coloring
Directions:
Mix salt and flour until smooth. Add enough water to make a smooth paste. Apply with a craft stick. If a tinted paint is desired, add food coloring to the mixture.
Suggestions for use:
1. Use salt paint to represent snow in a winter scene drawn with crayon.
2. Use salt paint as textured thick white wool on a sheep precut from white paper.

Play Clay

Ingredients:
3 cups flour
1½ cups salt
2 tablespoons cream of tartar
3 cups water
2 tablespoons vegetable oil
Food coloring

Directions:
Mix flour, salt, and cream of tartar in a large pan. Set aside. Mix together water, oil, and food coloring. Add liquid slowly to dry mixture. Mix well. Cook over a low heat stirring constantly. Cook until the mixture boils and becomes slightly transparent. The clay will form a solid ball at this stage. Cool and knead. Keep refrigerated in an airtight container. This clay will last for several months. *(No photo.)*
Suggestions for use:
This clay is for reuse and molding play. Provide the children with cookie cutters and small rolling pins which can be made from cutting an old broom handle or large dowel sticks into 6″ sections. Encourage children to mold objects into their own creations without the aid of the cookie cutters.

Glue Clay

Ingredients:
One part white glue
One part flour
One part cornstarch
Food coloring

Directions:
Mix all ingredients with a spoon. Knead until a clay-like consistency is reached. If the clay is dry, add a few additional drops of glue. If a tinted clay is desired, add food coloring to the glue before mixing with flour and cornstarch. Store in an airtight container at room temperature.

Mold clay into objects shaped from a single piece or roll out clay and cut into desired shapes with a table knife, small cookie cutter, or pill bottle. Air dry. If desired, decorate with tempera paints or waterbased markers.
Suggestions for use:
1. Make small refrigerator magnets by placing magnetic plastic tape to the back of finished piece.
2. Make a pendant or other small piece of jewelry.

Bubbles

Ingredients:
One part liquid dishwashing detergent
Three parts water
A small amount of sugar, liquid vegetable oil, or corn
  syrup
Food coloring

Directions:
Mix ingredients together. Detergents vary. If the water dilutes the soap too much and bubbles are not easily formed, add some more detergent.

Suggestions for use:
1. For variety add a small amount of food coloring to the bubble mixture.
2. For bubble blowers try some of the following:
   a. Use a rubber band to hold 6-8 straws together. Dip one end of the straw into the bubble solution and then blow through the other end of the straws.
   b. With a can opener remove both top and bottom from a metal can. Be sure that there are no sharp edges inside the can. Run the open can around the can opener several times to flatten any rough edges. Try a large coffee can to make large bubbles.
   c. Cut the plastic frame which held a six pack of soft drink cans together into one circle and two circle sections. Staple a one circle section to a two circle section making a three leaf clover shape. Staple a plastic drinking straw onto the bottom for a handle. *(Pictured.)*

Unleavened Bread

Ingredients:
1 cup flour
1/3 cup water

Directions:
Mix flour and water in a small bowl. Knead to a claylike consistency adding an additional 2 or 3 tablespoons of flour if necessary. Roll dough in flour and then roll out as thin as possible between two sheets of waxed paper. Place on a greased cookie sheet. Make pricks with a fork and score into small squares with a knife. Bake in a preheated oven at 475 degrees for about 10 minutes until the edges become golden brown. *(No photo.)*

Suggestions for use:
1. Use with lessons about the first Passover.
2. Use with lessons about the Last Supper.

Glue Paint

Ingredients:
White glue
Food coloring

Directions:
Mix food coloring into small amounts of white glue. Mix until colors are well blended. Apply with small brushes.

Suggestions for use:
1. Paint a scene or design onto a small glass or jar. Place a votive candle inside. *(Pictured.)*
2. Decorate the edges of a small mirror.
3. Spray paint the screw-on metal lid of a jar. Paint a design onto the jar with the glue paint. Use as a storage jar or plant a terrarium.

Salt Ink

Ingredients:
One part salt
One part hot water

Directions:
Stir salt and water. Let cool. All the salt will not dissolve. Dip a flat wooden toothpick into the saltwater. Print a message, memory verse, or draw a picture on a piece of paper with a smooth surface. As the salt ink dries it will almost disappear. To make the words or picture visible again, rub over the area with the point of a soft lead pencil. *(No photo.)*

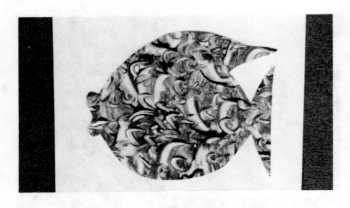

Chemical Gardens

Ingredients:
2 charcoal briquets
2 tablespoons salt
2 tablespoons water
2 tablespoons bluing
1 teaspoon ammonia
Food coloring

Directions:
Place briquets in a small container. Mix salt, water, bluing, and ammonia. Pour mixture over briquets. An optional few drops of food coloring can be placed onto the briquets. Crystals will begin to form in one hour and continue to grow for several days. Crystals will grow best when the air is not humid. *(No photo.)*

Window Paint

Ingredients:
Tempera - thick consistency
Liquid dishwashing detergent

Directions:
Add a small amount of detergent to the tempera. With a small amount of paint on brush, paint on the classroom windows. *(No photo.)*

Finger Paint

Ingredients:
Liquid laundry starch
Powdered tempera

Directions:
Mix well before placing on paper.
Suggestions for use:
1. Instead of plain paper, use a piece of wallpaper with a smooth surface.
2. After finger printed design has dried, cut paper into shape of fish, butterfly, leaf, etc.

INDEX